NINJA DOUBLE STACK AIR FRYER COOKBOOK:

Easy and Healthy Ninja Vertical Dual Drawer Air Fryer Recipes.

(Ninja Dual Zone Air Fryer Cookbook)

By
Oscar Wright

© Copyright by Oscar Wright 2024 - All rights reserved.

The content contained within this book may not be reproduced, duplicated or transmitted without direct written permission from the author or the publisher.

Under no circumstances will any blame or legal responsibility be held against the publisher, or author, for any damages, reparation, or monetary loss due to the information contained within this book. Either directly or indirectly. You are responsible for your own choices, actions, and results.

Legal Notice:
This book is copyright protected. This book is only for personal use. You cannot amend, distribute, sell, use, quote or paraphrase any part, or the content within this book, without the consent of the author or publisher.

Disclaimer Notice:
Please note the information contained within this document is for educational and entertainment purposes only. All effort has been executed to present accurate, up to date, and reliable, complete information. No warranties of any kind are declared or implied. Readers acknowledge that the author is not engaging in the rendering of legal, financial, medical or professional advice. The content within this book has been derived from various sources. Please consult a licensed professional before attempting any techniques outlined in this book.

By reading this document, the reader agrees that under no circumstances is the author responsible for any losses, direct or indirect, which are incurred as a result of the use of the information contained within this document, including, but not limited to, — errors, omissions, or inaccuracies.

CONTENTS

INTRODUCTION / 7
What is a Ninja Double Stack Air Fryer? / 8
Benefits and advantages of the Ninja Double Stack Air Fryer / 8
How to use the Ninja Double Stack XL air fryer / 9
Functions of Ninja Double Stack XL air fryer / 10

BREAKFAST RECIPES / 11
Banana Oatmeal Muffins / 12
Perfect Sweet Potato Hash / 12
Delicious Sausage Balls / 13
Healthy Cod Fritters / 13
Potato Sausage Hash Breakfast / 14
Healthy Frittata Cups / 14
French Toast Cups / 15
Ham Egg Bites / 15
Sweet Potato Fritters / 16
Crispy Potato with Pepper / 16

LUNCH RECIPES / 17
Juicy Chicken Breasts / 18
Stuffed Sweet Peppers / 18
Quick & Tender Steak Tips / 19
Crispy Crusted Haddock / 19
Pesto Fish Fillets / 20
Curried Cod Fillets / 20
Balsamic Vegetables / 21
Balsamic Broccoli & Brussels Sprouts / 21
Spinach Quinoa Patties / 22
Stuffed Aubergine / 22

APPETISER & SIDE DISHES / 23
Cinnamon Apple Chips / 24
Simple Roasted Parsnips / 24
Quick & Easy Mushrooms / 25
Perfect Aubergine / 25
Roasted Sweet Peppers / 26
Tasty Baby Potatoes / 26
Crispy Carrot Fries / 27
Delicious Garlic Bread / 27
Lemon Garlic Broccoli / 28
Roasted Nuts / 28

FISH & SEAFOOD RECIPES / 29

Perfect Salmon Bites / 30
Salmon Jerky / 30
Tasty Prawns / 31
Quick Salmon Belly / 31
Tender Salmon Steak / 32
Lemon Garlic Scallops / 32
Baked Tilapia / 33
Savory Crab Cakes / 33
Crispy Cod Fillets / 34
Easy Tuna Cakes / 34

POULTRY RECIPES / 35

Delicious Chicken Drumsticks / 36
Tasty Chicken Patties / 36
Chicken with Brussels Sprouts / 37
Crispy Crusted Chicken Drumsticks / 37
Tasty Turkey Wings / 38
Chicken Skewers / 38
Quick Chicken Fajita Skewers / 39
Curried Chicken Drumsticks / 39
Turkey Patties / 40
Quick Chicken with Veggies / 40
Chicken Thighs / 41
Juicy Chicken Bites / 41
Lemon Pepper Chicken Wings / 42
Flavourful Chicken Legs / 42
Turkey Meatballs / 43
Dijon Chicken Breast / 43
Turkey Mushroom Patties / 44
Stuffed Chicken Breast / 44
Chicken Stuffed Mini Peppers / 45
Chicken Jerky / 45

MEAT RECIPES 47

Meatballs / 48
Parmesan Pork Chops / 48
Quick Pork Chop Bites / 49
Quick Beef Skewers / 49
Steak Bites with Veggies / 50
Tasty Steak Strips / 50
Juicy Pork Chops / 51
Juicy Pork Meatballs / 51
Simple Lamb Skewers / 52
Pork Chops with Sprouts / 52
Steak with Vegetables / 53
Marinated Flank Steak / 53
Pork Belly Bites with Mushrooms / 54

Lemon Herb Lamb Chops / 54
Baked Beef Meatballs / 55
Steak with Potatoes / 55
Quick Steak Bites / 56
Sausage with Vegetables / 56
Pork Jerky / 57
Beef Jerky / 57

VEGETABLE RECIPES / 59

Healthy Root Vegetable / 60
Garlic Lime Courgette / 60
Roasted Mixed Vegetables / 61
Roasted Brussels Sprouts / 61
Crispy Broccoli Bites / 62
Roasted Cauliflower / 62
Sweet Potato Courgette Patties / 63
Aubergine Slices / 63
Green Bean Chips / 64
Beet Slices / 64

DESSERTS / 65

Cranberry Muffins / 66
Healthy Brownie Bites / 66
Chocolate Muffins / 67
Roasted Oranges / 67
Brazilan Pineapple Chunks / 68
Cinnamon Figs / 68
Lemon Muffins / 69
Green Apple Slices / 69
Peach Slices / 70
Healthy Oat Cookies / 70

CONCLUSION / 71

Bon Appetit!!!

Introduction

Thanks for joining us on this wonderful culinary adventure with the Ninja Double Stack XL Air Fryer! With these step-by-step recipes and secrets, I promise you it will not disappoint! No matter if you are a complete newcomer to using an air fryer or a master looking for some new inspiration. This book is as important to you as your air fryer.

The Ninja Double Stack XL Air Fryer is remarkable not just for its spaciousness but also for its unique layout that enables cooking on multiple levels. Imagine being able to cook several meals at once. Thanks to the Ninja air fryer, this dream is now a reality for home cooks who wish to make a variety of meals.
The following cookbook is filled with 100 recipes that present different ways of using the features of the Ninja Double Stack XL Air Fryer.

From breakfast, appetizers, and filling entrees to sweet desserts, the following recipes were developed to allow you to cook as many meals in the air fryer as possible. One will also find meals that respond to all preferences and dietary restrictions, meaning no one will stay hungry. Get ready to treat yourself to healthier, quick, and hassle-free meals for your family and friends. These dishes use very little oil and are health-sensitive without being flavorless!

In other words, turn the page, choose a recipe, and get cooking with your Ninja Double Stack XL Air Fryer. Discover new flavor combinations, play around with new ingredients, and relish in the satisfying, easy goodness that is cooking at home. Use this cookbook as your guide to see all the amazing meals you can make using just one epic appliance!

Enjoy your cooking!

What is a Ninja Double Stack Air Fryer?

The Ninja Double Stack XL Air Fryer is one of the unique designs of air fryers available on the market. This appliance features double baskets, and they stack on top of each other. It's basically like having two air fryers in one but in a much smaller package. Depending on your family or cooking needs, you can choose between two different size models, SL300 or SL400. Cooking two things simultaneously is a game changer.

This is one of the multifunctional air fryers. It comes with dual cooking zones and can air fry, roast, bake, max crisp, reheat, and dehydrate. Plus, each basket comes with a crisper plate and rack for more meal-making potential. Another feature is that it needs 30% less counter space than conventional air fryers, making it the ideal model for smaller kitchens. New users may also seamlessly operate the Ninja Double Stack XL air fryer due to its space-saving side-mounted control panel.

The air fryer, designed for small kitchens, is the first of its kind with a vertical stacking system, and it is at the vanguard of an innovative development in compact appliance design. This is one of the ideal devices for home chefs because it is simple to use, comes with several programs, and saves time and space.

Benefits and advantages of the Ninja Double Stack Air Fryer

The Ninja Double Stack XL Air Fryer comes with lots of benefits and advantages, which is why it stands out as a must-have kitchen gadget. Here are some benefits and advantages it includes:

1. Save Kitchen Counter-Top Space
It comes with a double-stacked drawer design that can save 30% of precious counter space that you would not enjoy with your traditional air fryer. It is a perfect choice for those people who have a small kitchen space.

2. Cooks Lots of Food into a Single Cooking Cycle
The Ninja Double Stacked XL makes it possible to have a full-sized oven meal in half the time. Using this air fryer, you can cook 4 different types of food in a single cooking cycle. It has enough room for 3.3lb chicken in each drawer. It is one of the best choices for your weekend parties.

3. Versatile Cooking Appliances
The Ninja Double Stacked XL air fryer offers versatile cooking functions such as air frying, roasting, baking, reheating, dehydrating, and max crisp in a single cooking appliance. This versatility helps users prepare a wide range of different recipes for both appetizers and main courses.

4. Offers Dual Cooking Zones
The appliance features independent temperature controls and offers flexibility to customize your cooking for each drawer, which means it allows you to cook different foods simultaneously

and air fry two foods at different temperatures in different settings. This flexibility improves cooking efficiency and is perfect for preparing a variety of meals.

5. Cut Down Your Cooking Time
The efficient heat distribution system and rapid airflow technology of the new air fryer reduces cooking time significantly so that you can eat your meals sooner. SYNC and MATCH settings allow you to finish cooking both zones at the same time.

6. Cook Healthy Food
Compared with traditional frying, your Ninja Double Stack XL air fryer uses 75 percent less oil for frying. Research has shown that reducing calorie intake can affect energy balance and metabolism, lowering the risk of fat-related health issues. Air frying your food is one of the healthy methods of cooking your food without changing the taste and texture like deep fried food.

How to use the Ninja Double Stack XL air fryer

The following step-by-step instructions will help you to use your Ninja Double Stack XL air fryer.

1. Initial Setup

- *Unpack and Inspect:* Unpack your Ninja Double Stack XL air fryer, and make sure that all components are present and in good condition.
- *Placement:* Place your air fryer on a flat, stable, heatproof surface away from water and heat sources.

2. Preparation Before Cooking

- *Wash and clean food baskets:* Before you use an air fryer for the first time, make sure both the food baskets are washed in warm and soapy water. Dry them thoroughly.

- *Preheat your air fryer:* Though it isn't always necessary, you can preheat the air fryer for three to five minutes to get better cooking results, especially when you cook frozen foods.

3. Load your Air Fryer

- *Prepare the Food:* Place your food in the basket. Always remember not to pack it too full, or you won't get air flowing properly around all the pieces. This will lead to uneven cooking results.
- *Insert the Baskets:* Carefully slide the baskets into the air fryer unit.

4. Setup your Cooking Preferences

- *Choose the Cooking Method:* Select the correct mode (like air fry, roast, bake, reheat, and dehydrate) as per your recipe requirements.
- *Set the Time and Temperature:* Use time and temperature settings to set the Cooking time and temperature in the cooking cycle as per your recipe needs.

5. Start Cooking Process

- *Begin cooking:* Press the start button to begin the actual cooking process. You can also monitor cooking progress as needed.
- *If applicable, use the SYNC or MATCH function:* Use the SYNC function to finish cooking both zones at the same time, or use the MATCH function to cook both zones with the same settings.

6. Monitor Your Food

- *Check your food periodically:* Open your air fryer occasionally to check the cooking progress and shake/stir the contents to get even cooking results.

7. Finish Cooking and Serving

- *End cooking:* The air fryer will notify you when the cooking time reaches zero. Wait for a minute or two after the completion cycle before removing the baskets to avoid steam burns.
- *Serve Food:* Take out the baskets and empty the food onto the plates. Now your food is ready to be served.

8. Cleaning and Maintenance

- *Cool down:* Make sure that the air fryer is properly cooled before cleaning.
- *Clean air fryer basket and interior:* Either wash the baskets with soapy water or put them in the dishwasher. The interior can be wiped with a damp cloth.

Functions of Ninja Double Stack XL air fryer

The Ninja Double Stack XL Air Fryer has many functions, making the tool versatile for cooking. Here are its primary functions:

1. Air Fry: In this function, hot air is circulated into a cooking chamber to cook food faster and with little or no oil. It is one of the healthier ways of cooking than traditional deep frying. This mode is ideal for making crispy foods like French fries, chicken wings, and more.

2. Max Crisp: This function is designed for rapid and even cooking of frozen food and makes your food super crispy. Therefore, this is perfect for breaded fish fillets or frozen fries.

3. Roast: This function is ideal for roasting a wide number of foods, including meat, vegetables, and other strong foods. This function makes your food tender and juicy on the inside while crispy and crunchy on the outside.

4. Bake: One of my favorite functions is to bake a cake, cookies, and other pastries using an air fryer. To get perfect and faster baking results, always preheat your air fryer before baking your food.

5. Dehydrate: This function is used to gently take away moisture from fruit, vegetables, and jerky to leave them dry. This function is ideal for preserving food for a longer period.

6. Reheat: This function allows you to warm up already cooked foods without losing their texture. This could not be possible in a microwave oven since it will dry up the foods after reheating.

7. Double Stack Pro: The double stack pro feature in an air fryer permits the cooking of 2 separate baskets of food at the same time, reducing the total cooking time.

8. SYNC: If your cooking settings, temperature, and timing in the zones are different, the SYNC function takes care of setting the time of another zone so that your meals in all cooking zones are ready at the same time.

9. MATCH: The MATCH button is used to transfer the cooking parameters from zone-1 to zone-2 automatically. If you are cooking a bunch of the same thing or a bunch of things at the same temperature, you can press this button.

Breakfast Recipes

Banana Oatmeal Muffins

Procedure of Cooking:

Cooking Period: 20 mins.

1. In a mixing bowl, add eggs, milk, mashed bananas, and maple syrup and mix until well combined.
2. Add oats and let sit for 5 minutes.
3. Add flour, baking powder, baking soda, and cinnamon and mix until just combined.
4. Spoon batter into silicone muffin molds.
5. Install a crisper plate in both drawers, then place half muffin molds in the zone 1 drawer and half in the zone 2 drawer, then insert the drawers into the unit.
6. Select zone 1, select Bake, set the temperature to 220 C, and set the time to 20 minutes.
7. Select the Match button to copy the zone 1 settings to zone 2.
8. Press the Start/Stop to begin cooking.
9. Serve and enjoy.

Ingredients Required:
Serving: 12

- Eggs - 2
- Ripe bananas, mashed - 3
- Cinnamon - 1 tsp
- Whole wheat flour - 180 g
- Rolled oats - 80 g
- Unsweetened almond milk - 120 ml
- Maple syrup - 118 ml
- Baking soda - 1/2 tsp
- Baking powder - 1 tsp
- Nutmeg - 1/8 tsp

Per Person: Calories 165, Carbs 31.73g, Fat 4.14g, Protein 5.17g

Perfect Sweet Potato Hash

Procedure of Cooking:

Cooking Period: 12 mins.

1. In a mixing bowl, toss sweet potatoes with paprika, Creole seasoning, olive oil, garlic, sweet pepper, and onion.
2. Install a crisper plate in both drawers, then add half sweet potato mixture in the zone 1 drawer and half in the zone 2 drawer, then insert the drawers into the unit.
3. Select zone 1, select Air Fry, set the temperature to 200 C, and set the time to 12 minutes.
4. Select the Match button to copy the zone 1 settings to zone 2.
5. Press the Start/Stop to begin cooking.
6. Serve and enjoy.

Ingredients Required:
Serving: 4

- Sweet potatoes, cut into 1-inch chunks - 3
- Dried chives - ½ tsp
- Paprika - ½ tsp
- Creole seasoning - 1 tsp
- Olive oil - 1 tbsp
- Garlic, minced - 1 tsp
- Red sweet pepper, chopped - 1
- Bacon slices, cooked & crumbled - 3
- Onion, diced - 1 medium

Per Person: Calories 159, Carbs 10.79g, Fat 11.56g, Protein 5.08g

Delicious Sausage Balls

Procedure of Cooking:

Cooking Period: 12 mins.

1. Add sausage and remaining ingredients into the mixing bowl and mix until well combined.
2. Make equal shapes of balls from the sausage mixture.
3. Install a crisper plate in both drawers, then place half of the meatballs in the zone 1 drawer and half in the zone 2 drawer, then insert the drawers into the unit.
4. Select zone 1, select Air Fry, set the temperature to 200 C, and set the time to 12 minutes.
5. Select the Match button to copy the zone 1 settings to zone 2.
6. Press the Start/Stop to begin cooking.
7. Serve and enjoy.

Ingredients Required:
Serving: 16 balls

- Egg, lightly beaten - 1
- Pork breakfast sausage - 450 g
- Cream cheese, softened - 30 g
- Cheddar cheese, shredded - 115 g
- Pepper
- Salt

Per Person: Calories 138, Carbs 1.36g, Fat 12g, Protein 5g

Healthy Cod Fritters

Procedure of Cooking:

Cooking Period: 15 mins.

1. Add fish and remaining ingredients into the mixing bowl and mix until well combined.
2. Make equal shapes of patties from the fish mixture.
3. Install a crisper plate in both drawers, then place half patties in the zone 1 drawer and half in the zone 2 drawer, and insert the drawers into the unit.
4. Select zone 1, select Air Fry, set the temperature to 200 C, and set the time to 15 minutes.
5. Select the Match button to copy the zone 1 settings to zone 2.
6. Press the Start/Stop to begin cooking.
7. Turn patties halfway through.
8. Serve and enjoy.

Ingredients Required:
Serving: 6

- Egg, lightly beaten - 1
- Cod fillet, flaked - 450 g
- All-purpose flour - 60 g
- Shallot, chopped - 1
- Garlic clove, minced - 1
- Chives, chopped - 10 g
- Carrot, grated - 1
- Pepper
- Salt

Per Person: Calories 413, Carbs 49.48g, Fat 22.89g, Protein 5.28g

Potato Sausage Hash Breakfast

Procedure of Cooking:
Cooking Period: 20 mins.

1. In a bowl, toss potatoes with olive oil, pepper, and salt.
2. In a separate bowl, add sausage, onions, and sweet peppers and mix well. Season with pepper and salt.
3. Add flour mixture into the egg mixture and mix until well combined.
4. Spoon batter into the silicone muffin molds.
5. Install a crisper plate in both drawers.
6. Add potatoes in the zone 1 drawer and sausage mixture in the zone 2 drawer, then insert the drawers into the unit.
7. Select zone 1, select Air Fry, set the temperature to 200 C, and set the time to 8 minutes.
8. Select zone 2, select Air Fry, set the temperature to 200 C, and set the time to 12 minutes.
9. Press the Start/Stop to begin cooking.
10. Serve and enjoy.

Ingredients Required:
Serving: 4

- Baby potatoes, quartered - 680 g
- Breakfast sausage, crumbled - 453 g
- Onion, chopped - 1/2
- Yellow sweet pepper, chopped - 1
- Red sweet pepper, chopped - 1
- Olive oil - 2 tbsp
- Pepper
- Salt

Per Person: Calories 472, Carbs 36g, Fat 39g, Protein 17g

Healthy Frittata Cups

Procedure of Cooking:
Cooking Period: 10 mins.

1. In a mixing bowl, whisk eggs with pepper and salt. Add onion, tomato, parsley, and basil and mix well.
2. Pour the egg mixture into the 12 silicone muffin molds.
3. Install a crisper plate in both drawers, then place half muffin molds in the zone 1 drawer and half in the zone 2 drawer, then insert the drawers into the unit.
4. Select zone 1, select Air Fry, set the temperature to 180 C, and set the time to 10 minutes.
5. Select the Match button to copy the zone 1 settings to zone 2.
6. Press the Start/Stop to begin cooking.
7. Serve and enjoy.

Ingredients Required:
Serving: 12 cups

- Eggs - 10
- Onion, chopped - 1 medium
- Tomato, chopped - 1 large
- Parsley, chopped - 12 g
- Basil, chopped - 12 g
- Pepper
- Salt

Per Person: Calories 138, Carbs 6.4g, Fat 8.2g, Protein 9.6g

French Toast Cups

Procedure of Cooking:
Cooking Period: 14 mins.

1. Add apple and butter into the bowl and microwave for 3 minutes.
2. In a bowl, mix bread cubes, sugar, and cornstarch.
3. In a separate bowl, whisk eggs with vanilla, cinnamon, maple syrup, and milk. Add apple and bread cubes and mix until well combined.
4. Spoon the apple bread mixture into the silicone muffin molds.
5. Install a crisper plate in both drawers, then place half muffin molds in the zone 1 drawer and half in the zone 2 drawer, then insert the drawers into the unit.
6. Select zone 1, select Air Fry, set the temperature to 180 C, and set the time to 14 minutes.
7. Select the Match button to copy the zone 1 settings to zone 2.
8. Press the Start/Stop to begin cooking.
9. Serve and enjoy.

Ingredients Required:
Serving: 6

- Eggs - 3
- Bread, cut into 1-inch cubes - 170 g
- Butter, melted - 1 tbsp
- Apple, peeled & cubed - 1
- Maple syrup - 2 tbsp
- Cinnamon - 1/2 tsp
- Vanilla - 1/2 tsp
- Milk - 160 ml
- Cornstarch - 1 tsp
- Brown sugar - 70 g

Per Person: Calories 232, Carbs 30.6g, Fat 8.63g, Protein 7.96g

Ham Egg Bites

Procedure of Cooking:
Cooking Period: 10 mins.

1. In a bowl, whisk eggs with milk, pepper, and salt.
2. Pour the egg mixture into the 8 silicone muffin molds. Sprinkle cheddar cheese and ham evenly over the top of the egg mixture.
3. Install a crisper plate in both drawers, then place half muffin molds in the zone 1 drawer and half in the zone 2 drawer, then insert the drawers into the unit.
4. Select zone 1, select Air Fry, set the temperature to 180 C, and set the time to 10 minutes.
5. Select the Match button to copy the zone 1 settings to zone 2.
6. Press the Start/Stop to begin cooking.
7. Serve and enjoy.

Ingredients Required:
Serving: 8

- Eggs - 6
- Ham, diced - 40 g
- Cheddar cheese, shredded - 60 g
- Milk - 1 tbsp
- Pepper
- Salt

Per Person: Calories 413, Carbs 49.48g, Fat 22.89g, Protein 5.28g

Sweet Potato Fritters

Procedure of Cooking:
Cooking Period: 8 mins.

1. Add shredded sweet potato into the bowl and cover with water. Set aside for 30 minutes.
2. Squeeze out excess liquid from shredded sweet potato.
3. Add shredded sweet potato and remaining ingredients into the bowl and mix until well combined.
4. Make equal shapes of patties from the sweet potato mixture.
5. Install a crisper plate in both drawers, then add half patties in the zone 1 drawer and half in the zone 2 drawer, then insert the drawers into the unit.
6. Select zone 1, select Air Fry, set the temperature to 200 C, and set the time to 8 minutes.
7. Select the Match button to copy the zone 1 settings to zone 2.
8. Press the Start/Stop to begin cooking.
9. Turn sweet potato patties halfway through.
10. Serve and enjoy.

Ingredients Required:
Serving: 12 fritters

- Egg, lightly beaten - 1
- Parmesan cheese, grated - 40 g
- Sweet potato, peeled & shredded - 1
- Bacon, cooked & crumbled - 2 tbsp
- Green onion, chopped - 2 tbsp
- Oregano - 1/2 tsp
- Onion powder - 1/2 tsp
- Flour - 30 g
- Pepper
- Salt

Per Person: Calories 45, Carbs 4.4g, Fat 2.13g, Protein 2.43g

Crispy Potato with Pepper

Procedure of Cooking:
Cooking Period: 15 mins.

1. In a bowl, toss potatoes with sweet pepper, onion, pepper, oil, garlic powder, paprika, and salt.
2. Install a crisper plate in both drawers, then add half the potato mixture in the zone 1 drawer and half in the zone 2 drawer, then insert the drawers into the unit.
3. Select zone 1, select Air Fry, set the temperature to 200 C, and set the time to 15 minutes.
4. Select the Match button to copy the zone 1 settings to zone 2.
5. Press the Start/Stop to begin cooking.
6. Stir the potato mixture halfway through.
7. Serve and enjoy.

Ingredients Required:
Serving: 4

- Potatoes, peel & cut into 1/2-inch pieces - 450 g
- Red sweet pepper, diced - 1
- Onion, diced - ½
- Olive oil - 2 tbsp
- Garlic powder - 1/2 tsp
- Paprika - 1/2 tsp
- Pepper
- Salt

Per Person: Calories 160, Carbs 22.72g, Fat 6.94g, Protein 2.84g

Lunch Recipes

Juicy Chicken Breasts

Procedure of Cooking:
Cooking Period: 18 mins.

1. In a small bowl, mix olive oil, garlic powder, paprika, oregano, pepper, and salt.
2. Brush chicken breasts with the oil spice mixture.
3. Install a crisper plate in both drawers, then place half chicken breasts in the zone 1 drawer and half in the zone 2 drawer, and insert the drawers into the unit.
4. Select zone 1, select Air Fry, set the temperature to 190 C, and set the time to 18 minutes.
5. Select the Match button to copy the zone 1 settings to zone 2.
6. Press the Start/Stop to begin cooking.
7. Turn chicken breasts halfway through.
8. Serve and enjoy.

Ingredients Required:
Serving: 4

- Chicken breasts, boneless & skinless - 4
- Garlic powder - 1 tsp
- Paprika - 1 tsp
- Oregano - 1 tsp
- Olive oil - 2 tbsp
- Pepper
- Salt

Per Serving: Calories 568, Carbs 2.11g, Fat 33g, Protein 31g

Stuffed Sweet Peppers

Procedure of Cooking:
Cooking Period: 25 mins.

1. In a bowl, mix quinoa, tomatoes, oregano, garlic, chickpeas, and salt.
2. Stuff the quinoa mixture into each sweet pepper half.
3. Install a crisper plate in both drawers, then place half the peppers in the zone 1 drawer and half in the zone 2 drawer, then insert the drawers into the unit.
4. Select zone 1, select Bake, set the temperature to 200 C, and set the time to 25 minutes.
5. Select the Match button to copy the zone 1 settings to zone 2.
6. Press the Start/Stop to begin cooking.
7. Top with crumbled cheese and serve.

Ingredients Required:
Serving: 6

- Sweet peppers, cut in half & remove seeds - 3
- Feta cheese, crumbled - 40 g
- Garlic, minced - 1 tsp
- Cooked quinoa - 60 g
- Chickpeas, rinsed - 60 g
- Cherry tomatoes, sliced - 120 g
- Oregano - 1/2 tsp
- Salt - 1/2 tsp

Per Person: Calories 418, Carbs 26.3g, Fat 31.11g, Protein 14.19g

Quick & Tender Steak Tips

Procedure of Cooking:
Cooking Period: 8 mins.

1. In a mixing bowl, add steak cubes and remaining ingredients and mix well. Cover and place in refrigerator for 30 minutes to marinate.
2. Install a crisper plate in both drawers, then place half steak cubes in the zone 1 drawer and half in the zone 2 drawer, then insert the drawers into the unit.
3. Select zone 1, select Air Fry, set the temperature to 200 C, and set the time to 8 minutes.
4. Select the Match button to copy the zone 1 settings to zone 2.
5. Press the Start/Stop to begin cooking.
6. Serve and enjoy.

Ingredients Required:
Serving: 4

- ESteak tips cubed - 900 g
- Garlic cloves, pressed - 4
- Mustard - 1 tsp
- Soy sauce, low-sodium - 2 tbsp
- Butter, melted - 2 tbsp
- Olive oil - 3 tbsp
- Pepper
- Salt

Per Person: Calories 679, Carbs 4.38g, Fat 37.13g, Protein 77.46g

Crispy Crusted Haddock

Procedure of Cooking:
Cooking Period: 10 mins.

1. In a shallow dish, whisk the egg.
2. Add flour to a plate.
3. In a separate shallow dish, breadcrumbs, seafood seasoning, pepper, and salt.
4. Brush fish fillets with oil. Coat each fish fillet with flour, dip it in egg, and finally coat it with breadcrumbs.
5. Install a crisper plate in both drawers, then place half of the fish fillets in the zone 1 drawer and half in the zone 2 drawer, then insert the drawers into the unit.
6. Select zone 1, select Air Fry, set the temperature to 180 C, and set the time to 10 minutes.
7. Select the Match button to copy the zone 1 settings to zone 2.
8. Press the Start/Stop to begin cooking.
9. Serve and enjoy.

Ingredients Required:
Serving: 4

- Egg - 1
- Haddock fillets - 450 g
- Seafood seasoning - 1 tsp
- Flour - 120 g
- Olive oil - 1 tbsp
- Breadcrumbs - 60 g
- Pepper
- Salt

Per Person: Calories 297, Carbs 31.15g, Fat 7g, Protein 25.21g

Pesto Fish Fillets

Procedure of Cooking:
Cooking Period: 10 mins.

1. Brush fish fillets with oil and season with pepper and salt.
2. Install a crisper plate in both drawers, then place half of the fish fillets in the zone 1 drawer and half in the zone 2 drawer, then insert the drawers into the unit.
3. Select zone 1, select Air Fry, set the temperature to 180 C, and set the time to 10 minutes.
4. Select the Match button to copy the zone 1 settings to zone 2.
5. Press the Start/Stop to begin cooking.
6. Add all pesto ingredients into the blender and blend until smooth.
7. Pour pesto over the cooked fish fillets and serve.

Ingredients Required:
Serving: 4

- Tilapia fillets - 4
- Olive oil - 2 tbsp
- Basil - 15 g
- Olive oil - 120 ml
- Parmesan cheese, shredded - 2 tbsp
- Pine nuts - 4 tbsp
- Garlic cloves - 2
- Pepper
- Salt

Per Serving: Calories 429, Carbs 2.04g, Fat 36.59g, Protein 24.47g

Curried Cod Fillets

Procedure of Cooking:
Cooking Period: 10 mins.

1. In a small bowl, mix butter, garlic powder, curry powder, paprika, pepper, and salt.
2. Brush fish fillets with butter mixture.
3. Install a crisper plate in both drawers, then place half fillets in the zone 1 drawer and half in the zone 2 drawer, and insert the drawers into the unit.
4. Select zone 1, select Air Fry, set the temperature to 180 C, and set the time to 10 minutes.
5. Select the Match button to copy the zone 1 settings to zone 2.
6. Press the Start/Stop to begin cooking.
7. Serve and enjoy.

Ingredients Required:
Serving: 4

- Cod fillets - 4
- Curry powder - 1/2 tsp
- Butter, melted - 2 tbsp
- Basil, sliced - 4 tbsp
- Garlic powder - 1/4 tsp
- Paprika - 1/4 tsp
- Pepper
- Salt

Per Person: Calories 138, Carbs 1.5g, Fat 6.33g, Protein 18.17g

Balsamic Vegetables

Procedure of Cooking:
Cooking Period: 12 mins.

1. In a mixing bowl, mix asparagus, squash, tomatoes, mushrooms, courgette, oil, mustard, vinegar, soy sauce, brown sugar, pepper, and salt.
2. Cover the bowl and place it in the refrigerator for 30 minutes.
3. Install a crisper plate in both drawers, then add half vegetable mixture in the zone 1 drawer and half in the zone 2 drawer, then insert the drawers into the unit.
4. Select zone 1, select Air Fry, set the temperature to 200 C, and set the time to 12 minutes.
5. Select the Match button to copy the zone 1 settings to zone 2.
6. Press the Start/Stop to begin cooking.
7. Stir vegetable mixture halfway through.
8. Serve and enjoy.

Ingredients Required:
Serving: 4

- Mushrooms, halved - 250 g
- Courgette, sliced - 1
- Asparagus, cut woody ends - 125 g
- Yellow squash, sliced - 1
- Grape tomatoes - 160 g
- Balsamic vinegar - 60 ml
- Olive oil - 60 ml
- Dijon mustard - 1 tbsp
- Soy sauce - 3 tbsp
- Brown sugar - 2 tbsp
- Pepper
- Salt

Per Person: Calories 396, Carbs 62.73g, Fat 16.53g, Protein 8.38g

Balsamic Broccoli & Brussels Sprouts

Procedure of Cooking:
Cooking Period: 10 mins.

1. In a bowl, toss broccoli florets and Brussels sprouts with vinegar, oil, pepper, and salt.
2. Install a crisper plate in both drawers, then add half the broccoli & Brussels sprout mixture in the zone 1 drawer and half in the zone 2 drawer, then insert the drawers into the unit.
3. Select zone 1, select Air Fry, set the temperature to 200 C, and set the time to 10 minutes.
4. Select the Match button to copy the zone 1 settings to zone 2.
5. Press the Start/Stop to begin cooking.
6. Stir the broccoli & Brussels sprout mixture halfway through.
7. Serve and enjoy.

Ingredients Required:
Serving: 4

- Broccoli florets - 350 g
- Brussels sprouts, halved - 200 g
- Balsamic vinegar - 2 tbsp
- Olive oil - 2 tbsp
- Pepper
- Salt

Per Person: Calories 95, Carbs 6.93g, Fat 7g, Protein 2.39g

Spinach Quinoa Patties

Procedure of Cooking:

Cooking Period: 10 mins.

1. In a large bowl, add quinoa and remaining ingredients and mix until well combined.
2. Make equal shapes of patties from the quinoa mixture.
3. Install a crisper plate in both drawers, then place half the patties in the zone 1 drawer and half in the zone 2 drawer, then insert the drawers into the unit.
4. Select zone 1, select Air Fry, set the temperature to 190 C, and set the time to 10 minutes.
5. Select the Match button to copy the zone 1 settings to zone 2.
6. Press the Start/Stop to begin cooking.
7. Serve and enjoy.

Ingredients Required:
Serving: 10

- Egg, lightly beaten - 1
- Spinach, chopped - 30 g
- Quinoa, cooked - 360 g
- Breadcrumbs - 60 g
- Parmesan cheese, grated - 25 g
- Milk - 60 ml
- Onion, chopped - 1 medium
- Carrot, peeled & shredded - 1/2
- Garlic, minced - 1 tsp
- Parsley, minced - 2 tbsp
- Pepper
- Salt

Per Person: Calories 160, Carbs 24.29g, Fat 3.97g, Protein 6.93g

Stuffed Aubergine

Procedure of Cooking:

Cooking Period: 12 mins.

1. In a bowl, mix together aubergine flesh, cheese, oregano, oil, sweet pepper, tomato, onion, garlic, paprika, and salt until well combined.
2. Stuff the filling in each aubergine half.
3. Install a crisper plate in both drawers, then place one aubergine half in the zone 1 drawer and another half in the zone 2 drawer, then insert the drawers into the unit.
4. Select zone 1, select Air fry, set the temperature to 190 C, and set the time to 12 minutes.
5. Select the Match button to copy the zone 1 settings to zone 2.
6. Press the Start/Stop to begin cooking.
7. Serve and enjoy.

Ingredients Required:
Serving: 2

- Aubergine, cut in half lengthwise & scoop out the flesh - 1 large
- Cheddar cheese, shredded - 3 tbsp
- Dried oregano - 1/3 tsp
- Olive oil - 1 tbsp
- Sweet pepper, chopped - 1/3
- Tomato, chopped - 1
- Onion, chopped - 1/2 small
- Garlic cloves, minced - 2
- Paprika - 1/3 tsp
- Salt - 1/4 tsp

Per Person: Calories 155, Carbs 22g, Fat 7g, Protein 3g

Appetiser & Side Dishes

Cinnamon Apple Chips

Procedure of Cooking:

Cooking Period: 20 mins.

1. In a mixing bowl, toss apple slices with cinnamon and sugar.
2. Install a crisper plate in both drawers, then place half the apple slices in the zone 1 drawer and the remaining half in the zone 2 drawer, then insert the drawers into the unit.
3. Select zone 1, select Air Fry, set the temperature to 150 C, and set the time to 20 minutes.
4. Select the Match button to copy the zone 1 settings to zone 2.
5. Press the Start/Stop to begin cooking.
6. Turn apple slices after 15 minutes.
7. Remove apple chips from the air fryer drawers and let them cool completely.
8. Serve and enjoy.

Ingredients Required:
Serving: 2

- Large apple, sliced into 1/8-inch-thick slices - 1
- Ground cinnamon - 1/2 tsp
- Sugar - 1 tbsp

Per Serving: Calories 75, Carbs 19.91g, Fat 0.2g, Protein 0.32g

Simple Roasted Parsnips

Procedure of Cooking:

Cooking Period: 15 mins.

1. In a bowl, toss parsnips with olive oil, pepper, and salt until well coated.
2. Install a crisper plate in both drawers, then place half of the parsnip pieces in the zone 1 drawer and half in the zone 2 drawer, then insert the drawers into the unit.
3. Select zone 1, select Air Fry, set the temperature to 200 C, and set the time to 15 minutes.
4. Select the Match button to copy the zone 1 settings to zone 2.
5. Press the Start/Stop to begin cooking.
6. Stir parsnips halfway through.
7. Serve and enjoy.

Ingredients Required:
Serving: 4

- Parsnips peeled & cut into equal pieces - 350 g
- Olive oil - 1 tbsp
- Pepper - 1/4 tsp
- Sea salt - 1 tsp

Per Person: Calories 93, Carbs 15.15g, Fat 3.64g, Protein 1.21g

Quick & Easy Mushrooms

Procedure of Cooking:

Cooking Period: 10 mins.

1. In a bowl, toss mushrooms with the remaining ingredients until well coated.
2. Install a crisper plate in both drawers, then add half mushrooms in the zone 1 drawer and half in the zone 2 drawer, then insert the drawers into the unit.
3. Select zone 1, select Air Fry, set the temperature to 180 C, and set the time to 10 minutes.
4. Select the Match button to copy the zone 1 settings to zone 2.
5. Press the Start/Stop to begin cooking.
6. Stir mushrooms halfway through.
7. Serve and enjoy.

Ingredients Required:
Serving: 2

- Mushrooms, cut in half - 400 g
- Worcestershire sauce - 1 tbsp
- Olive oil - 1 tbsp
- Dried rosemary - 1 sprig
- Pepper
- Salt

Per Person: Calories 669, Carbs 154.73g, Fat 8.83g, Protein 19.64g

Perfect Aubergine

Procedure of Cooking:

Cooking Period: 15 mins.

1. In a large mixing bowl, add aubergine strips and remaining ingredients and toss until well coated.
2. Install a crisper plate in both drawers, then place half aubergine strips in the zone 1 drawer and half in the zone 2 drawer, then insert the drawers into the unit.
3. Select zone 1, select Air Fry, set the temperature to 190 C, and set the time to 15 minutes.
4. Select the Match button to copy the zone 1 settings to zone 2.
5. Press the Start/Stop to begin cooking.
6. Stir aubergine strips halfway through.
7. Serve and enjoy.

Ingredients Required:
Serving: 4

- Aubergines, cut in half lengthwise, then into strips - 2
- Dried oregano - 1/2 tsp
- Onion powder - 1/2 tsp
- Garlic granules - 1 tsp
- Olive oil - 2 tbsp
- Pepper
- Salt

Per Person: Calories 215, Carbs 1.62g, Fat 12.53g, Protein 24.47g

Roasted Sweet Peppers

Procedure of Cooking:
Cooking Period: 12 mins.

1. In a mixing bowl, toss sweet pepper slices with oil, pepper, and salt until well coated.
2. Install a crisper plate in both drawers, then add half sweet pepper slices in the zone 1 drawer and half in the zone 2 drawer, then insert the drawers into the unit.
3. Select zone 1, select Air Fry, set the temperature to 200 C, and set the time to 12 minutes.
4. Select the Match button to copy the zone 1 settings to zone 2.
5. Press the Start/Stop to begin cooking.
6. Stir bell pepper halfway through.
7. Serve and enjoy.

Ingredients Required:
Serving: 6

- Red sweet peppers, sliced - 2
- Yellow sweet peppers, sliced - 2
- Olive oil - 1 tbsp
- Pepper
- Salt

Per Serving: Calories 35, Carbs 3.55g, Fat 2.33g, Protein 0.75g

Tasty Baby Potatoes

Procedure of Cooking:
Cooking Period: 15 mins.

1. In a mixing bowl, toss baby potatoes with the remaining ingredients until well coated.
2. Install a crisper plate in both drawers, then add half potatoes in the zone 1 drawer and half in the zone 2 drawer, then insert the drawers into the unit.
3. Select zone 1, select Air Fry, set the temperature to 200 C, and set the time to 15 minutes.
4. Select the Match button to copy the zone 1 settings to zone 2.
5. Press the Start/Stop to begin cooking.
6. Stir potatoes halfway through.
7. Serve and enjoy.

Ingredients Required:
Serving: 4

- Baby potatoes, cut in half - 500 g
- Paprika - 1/2 tsp
- Garlic granules - 1/2 tsp
- Italian seasoning - 1 tbsp
- Olive oil - 2 tbsp
- Pepper
- Salt

Per Person: Calories 169, Carbs 24.43g, Fat 6.93g, Protein 2.91g

Crispy Carrot Fries

Procedure of Cooking:
Cooking Period: 20 mins.

1. In a mixing bowl, toss carrot fries with oregano, basil, garlic powder, oil, pepper, and salt until well coated.
2. Install a crisper plate in both drawers, then add half carrot fries in the zone 1 drawer and half in the zone 2 drawer, then insert the drawers into the unit.
3. Select zone 1, select Air Fry, set the temperature to 180 C, and set the time to 20 minutes.
4. Select the Match button to copy the zone 1 settings to zone 2.
5. Press the Start/Stop to begin cooking.
6. Stir carrot fries halfway through.
7. Serve and enjoy.

Ingredients Required:
Serving: 4

- Carrots peeled & cut into fries shapes - 6
- Dried oregano - 1/2 tsp
- Dried basil - 1/2 tsp
- Garlic powder - 1 tsp
- Olive oil - 1 tbsp
- Pepper
- Salt

Per Person: Calories 75, Carbs 10.53g, Fat 3.63g, Protein 1.24g

Delicious Garlic Bread

Procedure of Cooking:
Cooking Period: 5 mins.

1. In a small bowl, mix butter, garlic, parsley, and sea salt.
2. Spread the butter mixture on top of each bread slice.
3. Install a crisper plate in both drawers, then place half bread slices in the zone 1 drawer and half in the zone 2 drawer, then insert the drawers into the unit.
4. Select zone 1, select Air Fry, set the temperature to 190 C, and set the time to 5 minutes.
5. Select the Match button to copy the zone 1 settings to zone 2.
6. Press the Start/Stop to begin cooking.
7. Serve and enjoy.

Ingredients Required:
Serving: 6

- Baguette, cut into slices - 240 g
- Parsley, chopped - 1 1/2 tbsp
- Garlic cloves, minced - 4
- Butter, unsalted & softened - 120 g
- Sea salt - 1 tsp

Per Person: Calories 218, Carbs 1g, Fat 20.62g, Protein 8.02g

Lemon Garlic Broccoli

Procedure of Cooking:
Cooking Period: 7 mins.

1. In a mixing bowl, toss broccoli florets with parmesan cheese, lemon juice, garlic, oil, pepper, and salt until well coated.
2. Install a crisper plate in both drawers, then add half of the broccoli florets in the zone 1 drawer and half in the zone 2 drawer, and then insert the drawers into the unit.
3. Select zone 1, select Air Fry, set the temperature to 180 C, and set the time to 7 minutes.
4. Select the Match button to copy the zone 1 settings to zone 2.
5. Press the Start/Stop to begin cooking.
6. Serve and enjoy.

Ingredients Required:
Serving: 2

- Broccoli head, cut into florets - 1
- Parmesan cheese, grated - 20 g
- Lemon juice - 1/2 lemon
- Garlic cloves, minced - 3
- Olive oil - 1 tbsp
- Pepper
- Salt

Per Person: Calories 138, Carbs 8.86g, Fat 9.58g, Protein 7.53g

Roasted Nuts

Procedure of Cooking:
Cooking Period: 25 mins.

1. In a mixing bowl, whisk together melted butter, maple syrup, cardamom, paprika, pepper, and salt. Add nuts and mix until well-coated.
2. Install a crisper plate in both drawers, then add half nuts in the zone 1 drawer and half in the zone 2 drawer, then insert the drawers into the unit.
3. Select zone 1, select Roast, set the temperature to 160 C, and set the time to 25 minutes.
4. Select the Match button to copy the zone 1 settings to zone 2.
5. Press the Start/Stop to begin cooking.
6. Stir nuts after every 10 minutes.
7. Transfer roasted nuts to the pan and let it cool completely.
8. Serve and enjoy.

Ingredients Required:
Serving: 16

- Aubergine, cut in half lengthwise & scoop out the Cashews - 130 g
- Pistachios - 60 g
- Pumpkin seeds - 30 g
- Walnuts - 120 g
- Pecans - 100 g
- Almonds - 140 g
- Paprika - 1/4 tsp
- Ground cardamom - 1 tsp
- Butter, melted - 2 tbsp
- Maple syrup - 2 tbsp
- Pepper
- Salt

Per Person: Calories 242, Carbs 9.69g, Fat 21.37g, Protein 6.63g

Fish & Seafood Recipes

Perfect Salmon Bites

Procedure of Cooking:
Cooking Period: 7 mins.

1. In a bowl, toss salmon chunks with paprika, oil, pepper, and salt until well coated.
2. Install a crisper plate in both drawers, then add half the salmon chunks in the zone 1 drawer and half in the zone 2 drawer, then insert the drawers into the unit.
3. Select zone 1, select Air Fry, set the temperature to 200 C, and set the time to 7 minutes.
4. Select the Match button to copy the zone 1 settings to zone 2.
5. Press the Start/Stop to begin cooking.
6. Flip the salmon chunks halfway through.
7. Serve and enjoy.

Ingredients Required:
Serving: 2

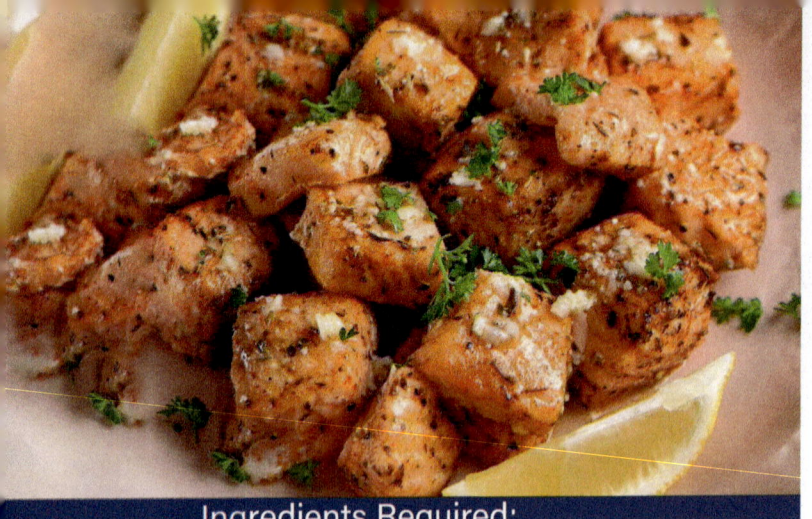

- Salmon - 240 g, cut into 1-inch chunks
- Paprika - 1/2 tsp
- Olive oil - 1 tbsp
- Pepper
- Salt

Per Serving: Calories 254, Carbs 2.45g, Fat 15.48g, Protein 25.29g

Salmon Jerky

Procedure of Cooking:
Cooking Period: 4 hours

1. In a mixing bowl, mix lemon juice, molasses, liquid smoke, pepper, and soy sauce.
2. Add salmon slices into the bowl and mix well. Cover and place in the refrigerator overnight.
3. Place a single layer of salmon slices in both the drawers. Then, install the crisper plate in the drawer on top of the salmon slices and place another layer of salmon slices on the crisper plate. Insert the drawers into the unit.
4. Select zone 1, select Dehydrate, set the temperature to 60 C, and set the time to 4 hours.
5. Select the Match button to copy the zone 1 settings to zone 2.
6. Press the Start/Stop to begin cooking.

Ingredients Required:
Serving: 6

- Salmon - 450 gm, cut into 1/4-inch slices
- Liquid smoke - 1/2 tsp
- Pepper - 1 tsp
- Molasses - 1 tbsp
- Soy sauce - 120 ml
- Fresh lemon juice - 1 tbsp

Per Person: Calories 190, Carbs 8.66g, Fat 9.28g, Protein 17.25g

Tasty Prawns

Procedure of Cooking:
Cooking Period: 8 mins.

1. In a mixing bowl, add prawns and remaining ingredients and mix well. Cover and set aside to marinate for 15 minutes.
2. Install a crisper plate in both drawers, then add half prawns in the zone 1 drawer and half in the zone 2 drawer, then insert the drawers into the unit.
3. Select zone 1, select Air Fry, set the temperature to 220 C, and set the time to 8 minutes.
4. Select the Match button to copy the zone 1 settings to zone 2.
5. Press the Start/Stop to begin cooking.
6. Serve and enjoy.

Ingredients Required:
Serving: 2

- King prawns - 400 g, peeled
- Lemon juice - 1/2 lemon
- Parsley - 15 g, chopped
- Olive oil - 2 tbsp
- Garlic cloves - 2, chopped
- Onion - 1/2, chopped
- Pepper
- Salt

Per Person: Calories 338, Carbs 42.26g, Fat 17.39g, Protein 15.65g

Quick Salmon Belly

Procedure of Cooking:
Cooking Period: 8 mins.

1. Season salmon belly strips with garlic, lemon zest, pepper, and salt.
2. Install a crisper plate in both drawers, then place half salmon belly strips in the zone 1 drawer and half in the zone 2 drawer, then insert the drawers into the unit.
3. Select zone 1, select Air Fry, set the temperature to 190 C, and set the time to 8 minutes.
4. Select the Match button to copy the zone 1 settings to zone 2.
5. Press the Start/Stop to begin cooking.
6. Drizzle with lemon juice and serve.

Ingredients Required:
Serving: 4

- Salmon belly strips - 450 g
- Garlic cloves - 4, minced
- Lemon zest - Grated zest of 1 lemon
- Lemon juice - Juice of 1 lemon
- Pepper
- Salt

Per Person: Calories 188, Carbs 3.71g, Fat 8.22g, Protein 23.86g

Tender Salmon Steak

Procedure of Cooking:
Cooking Period: 15 mins.

1. Place salmon steaks into the large mixing bowl. Mix remaining ingredients, pour over salmon steaks, and mix well.
2. Cover the bowl and place it in the refrigerator for 30 minutes to marinate the salmon steaks.
3. Install a crisper plate in both drawers, then place half salmon steaks in the zone 1 drawer and half in the zone 2 drawer, then insert the drawers into the unit.
4. Select zone 1, select Air Fry, set the temperature to 200 C, and set the time to 15 minutes.
5. Select the Match button to copy the zone 1 settings to zone 2.
6. Press the Start/Stop to begin cooking.
7. Flip salmon steaks halfway through.
8. Serve and enjoy.

Ingredients Required:
Serving: 4

- Salmon steaks - 4
- Lemon juice - Juice of 1 lemon
- Garlic cloves - 3, minced
- Soy sauce - 1 tbsp
- Olive oil - 1 tbsp
- Brown sugar - 1 tsp
- Pepper
- Salt

Per Serving: Calories 209, Carbs 4.76g, Fat 11.33g, Protein 21.33g

Lemon Garlic Scallops

Procedure of Cooking:
Cooking Period: 5 mins.

1. In a bowl, mix scallops, olive oil, tarragon, garlic, pepper, and salt until well coated.
2. Install a crisper plate in both drawers, then place half the scallops in the zone 1 drawer and half in the zone 2 drawer, then insert the drawers into the unit.
3. Select zone 1, select Air Fry, set the temperature to 200 C, and set the time to 5 minutes.
4. Select the Match button to copy the zone 1 settings to zone 2.
5. Press the Start/Stop to begin cooking.
6. Drizzle lemon juice over scallops and serve.

Ingredients Required:
Serving: 4

- Sea scallops - 450 g
- Olive oil - 2 tbsp
- Tarragon - 1/2 tbsp, minced
- Garlic cloves - 2, minced
- Lemon juice - Juice of 1 lemon
- Pepper
- Salt

Per Person: Calories 224, Carbs 2.39g, Fat 12.47g, Protein 26.3g

Baked Tilapia

Procedure of Cooking:
Cooking Period: 10 mins.

1. Season fish fillets with pepper and salt. Sprinkle herb breadcrumbs over each fish fillet and drizzle with melted butter.
2. Install a crisper plate in both drawers, then place half fish fillet in the zone 1 drawer and half in the zone 2 drawer, then insert the drawers into the unit.
3. Select zone 1, select Bake, set the temperature to 200 C, and set the time to 10 minutes.
4. Select the Match button to copy the zone 1 settings to zone 2.
5. Press the Start/Stop to begin cooking.
6. Serve and enjoy.

Ingredients Required:
Serving: 4

- Tilapia fillets - 4
- Herbed breadcrumbs - 75 gm
- Butter - 2 tbsp, melted
- Pepper
- Salt

Per Person: Calories 167, Carbs 1.13g, Fat 7.75g, Protein 23.58g

Savory Crab Cakes

Procedure of Cooking:
Cooking Period: 10 mins.

1. In a large bowl, add crabmeat and remaining ingredients and mix until well combined.
2. Make equal shapes of patties from the crabmeat mixture.
3. Install a crisper plate in both drawers, then place half the patties in the zone 1 drawer and half in the zone 2 drawer, and then insert the drawers into the unit.
4. Select zone 1, select Air Fry, set the temperature to 180 C, and set the time to 10 minutes.
5. Select the Match button to copy the zone 1 settings to zone 2.
6. Press the Start/Stop to begin cooking.
7. Serve and enjoy.

Ingredients Required:
Serving: 8

- Eggs - 2, lightly beaten
- Lump crabmeat - 900 g
- Cajun seasoning - 2 tbsp
- Worcestershire sauce - 2 tbsp
- Red bell pepper - 1, chopped
- Green onion - 4 tbsp, sliced
- All-purpose flour - 60 g
- Breadcrumbs - 60 g
- Mayonnaise - 115 g

Per Person: Calories 474, Carbs 52.56g, Fat 10.62g, Protein 47.05g

Crispy Cod Fillets

Procedure of Cooking:
Cooking Period: 10 mins.

1. In a small bowl, mix olive oil, garlic powder, paprika, pepper, and salt.
2. Brush cod fillets with olive oil mixture.
3. Install a crisper plate in both drawers, then place half the cod fillets in the zone 1 drawer and half in the zone 2 drawer, then insert the drawers into the unit.
4. Select zone 1, select Air Fry, set the temperature to 200 C, and set the time to 10 minutes.
5. Select the Match button to copy the zone 1 settings to zone 2.
6. Press the Start/Stop to begin cooking.
7. Serve and enjoy.

Ingredients Required:
Serving: 4

- Cod fillets - 4, 150 g each
- Garlic powder - 1 tsp
- Paprika - 1 tsp
- Olive oil - 2 tbsp
- Pepper
- Salt

Per Person: Calories 148, Carbs 1.94g, Fat 7.33g, Protein 18.15g

Easy Tuna Cakes

Procedure of Cooking:
Cooking Period: 12 mins.

1. In a mixing bowl, add drained tuna and remaining ingredients and mix until well combined.
2. Make equal shapes of patties from the tuna mixture.
3. Install a crisper plate in both drawers, then place half of the patties in the zone 1 drawer and half in the zone 2 drawer, then insert the drawers into the unit.
4. Select zone 1, select Air Fry, set the temperature to 190 C, and set the time to 12 minutes.
5. Select the Match button to copy the zone 1 settings to zone 2.
6. Press the Start/Stop to begin cooking.
7. Flip the tuna patties halfway through.
8. Serve and enjoy.

Ingredients Required:
Serving: 12

- Aubergine, cut in half lengthwise & scoop out the Eggs - 2, lightly beaten
- Can tuna - 680 g, drained
- Onion - 1/2, diced
- Mayonnaise - 4 tbsp
- Seasoned breadcrumbs - 45 g

Per Person: Calories 108, Carbs 4.41g, Fat 3.75g, Protein 13.19g

Poultry Recipes

Delicious Chicken Drumsticks

Procedure of Cooking:
Cooking Period: 20 mins.

1. Add chicken drumsticks and remaining ingredients into the mixing bowl and mix well.
2. Install a crisper plate in both drawers, then add half the chicken drumsticks in the zone 1 drawer and half in the zone 2 drawer, then insert the drawers into the unit.
3. Select zone 1, select Air Fry, set the temperature to 200 C, and set the time to 20 minutes.
4. Select the Match button to copy the zone 1 settings to zone 2.
5. Press the Start/Stop to begin cooking.
6. Flip the chicken drumsticks halfway through.
7. Serve and enjoy.

Ingredients Required:
Serving: 4

- Chicken drumsticks - 8
- Garlic granules - 1 tsp
- Paprika - 1 tbsp
- Olive oil - 2 tbsp
- Pepper
- Salt

Per Person: Calories 489, Carbs 2.5g, Fat 30.92g, Protein 47.52g

Tasty Chicken Patties

Procedure of Cooking:
Cooking Period: 15 mins.

1. Heat olive oil in a pan over medium heat.
2. Add onion to the pan and sauté for 5 minutes. Transfer sautéed onion to the mixing bowl.
3. Add chicken and remaining ingredients to the bowl and mix until well combined.
4. Make equal shapes of patties from the chicken mixture.
5. Install a crisper plate in both drawers, then place half the patties in the zone 1 drawer and half in the zone 2 drawer, then insert the drawers into the unit.
6. Select zone 1, select Air Fry, set the temperature to 200 C, and set the time to 10 minutes.
7. Select the Match button to copy the zone 1 settings to zone 2.
8. Press the Start/Stop to begin cooking.
9. Flip patties halfway through.
10. Serve and enjoy.

Ingredients Required:
Serving: 8

- Egg, lightly beaten - 1
- Ground chicken - 500 g
- Breadcrumbs - 60 g
- Fresh herbs, chopped - 2 tbsp
- Courgette, grated - 1
- Carrot, grated - 1
- Onion, diced - 1
- Olive oil - 2 tsp
- Pepper
- Salt

Per Person: Calories 179, Carbs 4.11g, Fat 11.88g, Protein 13.37g

Chicken with Brussels Sprouts

Procedure of Cooking:
Cooking Period: 20 mins.

1. Add chicken and all marinade ingredients into the large bowl and mix well. Cover the bowl and place it in the refrigerator overnight to marinate the chicken.
2. In a bowl, mix marinated chicken, Brussels sprouts, oil, pepper, and salt.
3. Install a crisper plate in both drawers, then place half of the chicken sprout mixture in the zone 1 drawer and half in the zone 2 drawer, then insert the drawers into the unit.
4. Select zone 1, select Bake, set the temperature to 200 C, and set the time to 30 minutes.
5. Select the Match button to copy the zone 1 settings to zone 2.
6. Press the Start/Stop to begin cooking.
7. Stir the chicken sprout mixture halfway through.
8. Serve and enjoy.

Ingredients Required:
Serving: 4

- Chicken thighs, boneless - 8
- Brussels sprouts, trimmed & halved - 680 g
- Olive oil - 2 tsp
- Pepper
- Salt

For marinade:

- Parsley, chopped - 2 tbsp
- Garlic, minced - 1 tsp
- Olive oil - 2 tbsp
- Dijon mustard - 1 tbsp
- Lemon juice - 2 tbsp
- Salt - 1/2 tbsp

Per Person: Calories 636, Carbs 17g, Fat 45.56g, Protein 41.73g

Crispy Crusted Chicken Drumsticks

Procedure of Cooking:
Cooking Period: 20 mins.

1. Put 15 ml of the oil, lemon juice, lemon zest, dried Add chicken drumsticks and buttermilk into the zip-lock bag. Seal the bag and place it in the refrigerator for 50 minutes.
2. In a shallow bowl, mix breadcrumbs, chicken seasoning, pepper, and salt.
3. Coat each chicken drumstick with the breadcrumb mixture.
4. Install a crisper plate in both drawers, then place half chicken drumsticks in the zone 1 drawer and half in the zone 2 drawer, then insert the drawers into the unit.
5. Select zone 1, select Air Fry, set the temperature to 200 C, and set the time to 20 minutes.
6. Select the Match button to copy the zone 1 settings to zone 2.
7. Press the Start/Stop to begin cooking.
8. Flip the chicken drumsticks halfway through.
9. Serve and enjoy.

Ingredients Required:
Serving: 4

- Chicken drumsticks - 1350 g
- Buttermilk - 60 ml
- Chicken seasoning - 2 tsp
- Breadcrumbs - 60 g
- Pepper
- Salt

Per Person: Calories 554, Carbs 7.36g, Fat 19.03g, Protein 84.55g

Tasty Turkey Wings

Procedure of Cooking:
Cooking Period: 33 mins.

1. In a small bowl, mix the poultry seasoning, paprika, thyme, oregano, garlic powder, pepper, and salt.
2. Brush the turkey wings with oil and rub them with the spice mixture.
3. Install a crisper plate in both drawers, then place half the turkey wings in the zone 1 drawer and half in the zone 2 drawer, then insert the drawers into the unit.
4. Select zone 1, select Air Fry, set the temperature to 200 C, and set the time to 35 minutes.
5. Select the Match button to copy the zone 1 settings to zone 2.
6. Press the Start/Stop to begin cooking.
7. Flip the turkey wings halfway through.
8. Serve and enjoy.

Ingredients Required:
Serving: 4

- Turkey wings - 1350 g
- Ground oregano - 1 tsp
- Ground thyme - 1 tsp
- Poultry seasoning - 2 tsp
- Canola oil - 1 tbsp
- Smoked paprika - 1 tsp
- Garlic powder - 1 tsp
- Pepper
- Salt

Per Person: Calories 543, Carbs 2.65g, Fat 10.74g, Protein 102.98g

Chicken Skewers

Procedure of Cooking:
Cooking Period: 10 mins.

1. Thread chicken pieces, tomatoes, and courgette onto the skewers.
2. Brush chicken skewers with oil and season with pepper and salt.
3. Install a crisper plate in both drawers, then place half the chicken skewers in the zone 1 drawer and half in the zone 2 drawer, then insert the drawers into the unit.
4. Select zone 1, select Air Fry, set the temperature to 200 C, and set the time to 10 minutes.
5. Select the Match button to copy the zone 1 settings to zone 2.
6. Press the Start/Stop to begin cooking.
7. Serve and enjoy.

Ingredients Required:
Serving: 6

- Chicken breast, cut into 1-inch pieces - 450 g
- Grape tomatoes - 160 g
- Courgette, cut into small pieces - 1 small
- Olive oil - 1 tbsp
- Pepper
- Salt

Per Person: Calories 171, Carbs 5.32g, Fat 9.31g, Protein 16.14g

Quick Chicken Fajita Skewers

Procedure of Cooking:
Cooking Period: 8 mins.

1. In a bowl, mix chicken, garlic powder, oil, cumin, chili powder, paprika, parsley flakes, oregano, lime juice, pepper, and salt. Cover and set aside for 30 minutes.
2. Thread marinated chicken pieces, onion, and sweet pepper onto the skewers.
3. Install a crisper plate in both drawers, then place half chicken skewers in the zone 1 drawer and half in the zone 2 drawer, then insert the drawers into the unit.
4. Select zone 1, select Air Fry, set the temperature to 180 C, and set the time to 8 minutes.
5. Select the Match button to copy the zone 1 settings to zone 2.
6. Press the Start/Stop to begin cooking.
7. Serve and enjoy.

Ingredients Required:
Serving: 4

- Chicken breasts, cut into small pieces - 450 g
- Onion, cut into pieces - 1 large
- Red sweet pepper, cut into pieces - 1
- Garlic powder - 1 tsp
- Olive oil - 2 tbsp
- Ground cumin - 1 tsp
- Paprika - 1 tsp
- Parsley flakes - 1 tsp
- Oregano - 1 tsp
- Chili powder - 1 tsp
- Fresh lime juice - 1 tbsp
- Pepper
- Salt

Per Person: Calories 200, Carbs 9.83g, Fat 9.23g, Protein 20.78g

Curried Chicken Drumsticks

Procedure of Cooking:
Cooking Period: 15 mins.

1. In a mixing bowl, add chicken drumsticks, curry powder, oil, garlic powder, pepper, and salt and toss to coat.
2. Install a crisper plate in both drawers, then place half of the chicken drumsticks in the zone 1 drawer and half in the zone 2 drawer, then insert the drawers into the unit.
3. Select zone 1, select Air Fry, set the temperature to 190 C, and set the time to 15 minutes.
4. Select the Match button to copy the zone 1 settings to zone 2.
5. Press the Start/Stop to begin cooking.
6. Flip the chicken drumsticks halfway through.
7. Serve and enjoy.

Ingredients Required:
Serving: 4

- Chicken drumsticks - 450 g
- Curry powder - 2 tsp
- Garlic powder - 1/2 tsp
- Olive oil - 2 tbsp
- Pepper
- Salt

Per Person: Calories 240, Carbs 1.91g, Fat 13.08g, Protein 28.02g

Turkey Patties

Procedure of Cooking:
Cooking Period: 14 mins.

1. In a bowl, mix ground turkey, egg white, Worcestershire sauce, basil, oregano, pepper, and salt until well combined.
2. Make equal shapes of patties from the turkey mixture.
3. Install a crisper plate in both drawers, then place half of the patties in the zone 1 drawer and half in the zone 2 drawer, then insert the drawers into the unit.
4. Select zone 1, select Air Fry, set the temperature to 180 C, and set the time to 14 minutes.
5. Select the Match button to copy the zone 1 settings to zone 2.
6. Press the Start/Stop to begin cooking.
7. Turn the patties halfway through.
8. Serve and enjoy.

Ingredients Required:
Serving: 4

- Egg white - 1
- Ground turkey – 450 g
- Worcestershire sauce - 2 tbsp
- Dried basil - 1/2 tsp
- Dried oregano - 1/2 tsp
- Pepper
- Salt

Per Person: Calories 184, Carbs 2.91g, Fat 8.72g, Protein 23.42g

Quick Chicken with Veggies

Procedure of Cooking:
Cooking Period: 10 mins.

1. In a bowl, toss chicken, vegetables, garlic powder, garlic, Italian seasoning, oil, chili powder, pepper, and salt until well coated.
2. Install a crisper plate in both drawers, then add half chicken vegetable mixture in the zone 1 drawer and half in the zone 2 drawer, then insert the drawers into the unit.
3. Select zone 1, select Air Fry, set the temperature to 200 C, and set the time to 10 minutes.
4. Select the Match button to copy the zone 1 settings to zone 2.
5. Press the Start/Stop to begin cooking.
6. Stir chicken vegetable mixture halfway through.
7. Serve and enjoy.

Ingredients Required:
Serving: 4

- Chicken breast, boneless & cut into pieces - 450 g
- Frozen mix vegetables – 300 g
- Garlic cloves, minced - 3
- Olive oil - 1 tbsp
- Italian seasoning - 1 tbsp
- Chili powder - 1/2 tsp
- Garlic powder - 1/2 tsp
- Pepper
- Salt

Per Person: Calories 204, Carbs 16.1g, Fat 5.67g, Protein 22.31g

Chicken Thighs

Procedure of Cooking:
Cooking Period: 12 mins.

1. In a mixing bowl, mix chicken thighs with oil, garlic powder, chili powder, cumin, pepper, and salt until well coated.
2. Install a crisper plate in both drawers, then place half of the chicken thighs in the zone 1 drawer and half in the zone 2 drawer, then insert the drawers into the unit.
3. Select zone 1, select Air Fry, set the temperature to 200 C, and set the time to 12 minutes.
4. Select the Match button to copy the zone 1 settings to zone 2.
5. Press the Start/Stop to begin cooking.
6. Turn the chicken thighs halfway through.
7. Serve and enjoy.

Ingredients Required:
Serving: 8

- Chicken thighs, boneless & skinless - 900 g
- Chili powder - 2 tsp
- Olive oil - 2 tsp
- Garlic powder - 1 tsp
- Ground cumin - 1 tsp
- Pepper
- Salt

Per Person: Calories 395, Carbs 17.4g, Fat 26.75g, Protein 21.47g

Juicy Chicken Bites

Procedure of Cooking:
Cooking Period: 20 mins.

1. Add chicken chunks and remaining ingredients into the mixing bowl and mix well. Cover and place in a refrigerator overnight.
2. Install a crisper plate in both drawers, then place half of the chicken chunks in the zone 1 drawer and half in the zone 2 drawer, then insert the drawers into the unit.
3. Select zone 1, select Air Fry, set the temperature to 190 C, and set the time to 20 minutes.
4. Select the Match button to copy the zone 1 settings to zone 2.
5. Press the Start/Stop to begin cooking.
6. Stir chicken halfway through.
7. Serve and enjoy.

Ingredients Required:
Serving: 4

- Chicken thighs, cut into chunks - 90 g
- Fresh lemon juice - 60 ml
- White pepper - 1/4 tsp
- Olive oil - 2 tbsp
- Onion powder - 1/2 tsp
- Garlic powder - 1/2 tsp
- Pepper
- Salt

Per Person: Calories 828, Carbs 35.01g, Fat 57.72g, Protein 42.7g

Lemon Pepper Chicken Wings

Procedure of Cooking:
Cooking Period: 20 mins.

1. In a bowl, toss chicken wings with oil, lemon zest, peppercorns, and garlic salt until well coated.
2. Install a crisper plate in both drawers, then add half of the chicken wings in the zone 1 drawer and half in the zone 2 drawer, then insert the drawers into the unit.
3. Select zone 1, select Air Fry, set the temperature to 180 C, and set the time to 20 minutes.
4. Select the Match button to copy the zone 1 settings to zone 2.
5. Press the Start/Stop to begin cooking.
6. Turn the chicken wings halfway through.
7. Serve and enjoy.

Ingredients Required:
Serving: 4

- Chicken wings - 900 g
- Black peppercorns, crushed - 2 tsp
- Olive oil - 1 tbsp
- Lemon zest, grated - 3 tsp
- Garlic salt - 1 tsp

Per Person: Calories 511, Carbs 8.25g, Fat 32.12g, Protein 44.7g

Flavourful Chicken Legs

Procedure of Cooking:
Cooking Period: 20 mins.

1. Add chicken legs and remaining ingredients into the large mixing bowl and mix well. Cover and place in refrigerator for 2 hours.
2. Install a crisper plate in both drawers, then place half of the chicken legs in the zone 1 drawer and half in the zone 2 drawer, then insert the drawers into the unit.
3. Select zone 1, select Air Fry, set the temperature to 190 C, and set the time to 20 minutes.
4. Select the Match button to copy the zone 1 settings to zone 2.
5. Press the Start/Stop to begin cooking.
6. Turn the chicken legs halfway through.
7. Serve and enjoy.

Ingredients Required:
Serving: 6

- Chicken legs - 6
- Garlic powder - 1 tsp
- Onion powder - 1 tsp
- Ground mustard - 1 tsp
- Olive oil - 1 tbsp
- Cayenne - 1/4 tsp
- Smoked paprika - 1 tsp
- Brown sugar - 3 tbsp
- Pepper
- Salt

Per Person: Calories 347, Carbs 1.75g, Fat 13.64g, Protein 51.2g

Turkey Meatballs

Procedure of Cooking:
Cooking Period: 10 mins.

1. In a mixing bowl, add meat and remaining ingredients and mix until well combined.
2. Make equal shapes of balls from the meat mixture.
3. Install a crisper plate in both drawers, then place half of the meatballs in the zone 1 drawer and half in the zone 2 drawer, then insert the drawers into the unit.
4. Select zone 1, select Air Fry, set the temperature to 200 C, and set the time to 10 minutes.
5. Select the Match button to copy the zone 1 settings to zone 2.
6. Press the Start/Stop to begin cooking.
7. Serve and enjoy.

Ingredients Required:
Serving: 4

- Egg, lightly beaten - 1
- Ground turkey - 450 g
- Parsley, minced - 2 tbsp
- Bell pepper, chopped - 1/2
- Mushrooms, diced - 50 g
- Fresh thyme, minced - 1 tsp
- Pepper
- Salt

Per Person: Calories 210, Carbs 2.41g, Fat 11.18g, Protein 25.28g

Dijon Chicken Breast

Procedure of Cooking:
Cooking Period: 20 mins.

1. In a shallow dish, mix breadcrumbs, pepper, and salt.
2. In a separate shallow dish, mix Dijon mustard and maple syrup.
3. Dip each chicken breast in the maple syrup mixture and coat with breadcrumbs.
4. Install a crisper plate in both drawers, then place half chicken breast in the zone 1 drawer and half in the zone 2 drawer, then insert the drawers into the unit.
5. Select zone 1, select Air Fry, set the temperature to 180 C, and set the time to 20 minutes.
6. Select the Match button to copy the zone 1 settings to zone 2.
7. Press the Start/Stop to begin cooking.
8. Serve and enjoy.

Ingredients Required:
Serving: 4

- Chicken breast, boneless & halves - 4
- Maple syrup - 80 ml
- Breadcrumbs - 60 g
- Dijon mustard - 120 g
- Pepper
- Salt

Per Person: Calories 629, Carbs 26.78g, Fat 28.8g, Protein 63.44g

Turkey Mushroom Patties

Procedure of Cooking:
Cooking Period: 15 mins.

1. Add ground turkey and remaining ingredients into the mixing bowl and mix until well combined.
2. Make equal shapes of patties from the turkey mixture.
3. Install a crisper plate in both drawers, then place half of the patties in the zone 1 drawer and half in the zone 2 drawer, then insert the drawers into the unit.
4. Select zone 1, select Air Fry, set the temperature to 190 C, and set the time to 15 minutes.
5. Select the Match button to copy the zone 1 settings to zone 2.
6. Press the Start/Stop to begin cooking.
7. Turn the patties halfway through.
8. Serve and enjoy.

Ingredients Required:
Serving: 5

- Ground turkey - 450 g
- Mushrooms, finely chopped - 8
- Worcestershire sauce - 1 tbsp
- Cilantro, chopped - 15 g
- Onion powder - 1 tsp
- Garlic powder - 1 tsp
- Pepper
- Salt

Per Person: Calories 151, Carbs 3.31g, Fat 7.07g, Protein 19.05g

Stuffed Chicken Breast

Procedure of Cooking:
Cooking Period: 30 mins.

1. In a mixing bowl, mix spinach, feta, oregano, garlic, pepper, and salt.
2. Stuff each chicken breast with the spinach mixture and secure it with toothpicks.
3. Install a crisper plate in both drawers, then place half of the chicken breasts in the zone 1 drawer and half in the zone 2 drawer, then insert the drawers into the unit.
4. Select zone 1, select Bake, set the temperature to 190 C, and set the time to 30 minutes.
5. Select the Match button to copy the zone 1 settings to zone 2.
6. Press the Start/Stop to begin cooking.
7. Serve and enjoy.

Ingredients Required:
Serving: 4

- Chicken breasts, boneless, skinless & cut a pocket into each chicken breast - 4
- Feta cheese, crumbled - 75 g
- Fresh spinach, chopped - 30 g
- Dried oregano - 1 tsp
- Garlic, minced - 1 tsp
- Pepper
- Salt

Per Person: Calories 556, Carbs 2.51g, Fat 30.88g, Protein 63.64g

Chicken Stuffed Mini Peppers

Procedure of Cooking:
Cooking Period: 15 mins.

1. In a mixing bowl, mix shredded chicken, parmesan cheese, cream cheese, paprika, garlic, basil, green onion, parsley, pepper, and salt until well combined.
2. Stuff chicken mixture into each pepper half.
3. Install a crisper plate in both drawers, then place half of the peppers in the zone 1 drawer and half in the zone 2 drawer, then insert the drawers into the unit.
4. Select zone 1, select Bake, set the temperature to 190 C, and set the time to 15 minutes.
5. Select the Match button to copy the zone 1 settings to zone 2.
6. Press the Start/Stop to begin cooking.
7. Serve and enjoy.

Ingredients Required:
Serving: 8

- Mini peppers, cut lengthwise & remove seeds - 8
- Cooked chicken, shredded - 90 g
- Basil leaves, chopped - 5
- Green onion, chopped - 1
- Paprika - 1/2 tsp
- Garlic, minced - 1/2 tsp
- Parsley, chopped - 1 tbsp
- Parmesan cheese, shredded - 2 tbsp
- Cream cheese, softened - 4 tbsp
- Pepper
- Salt

Per Person: Calories 263, Carbs 7.02g, Fat 23.83g, Protein 8.69g

Chicken Jerky

Procedure of Cooking:
Cooking Period: 7 hours

1. Add chicken slices and remaining ingredients into the zip-lock bag, seal the bag, and place in the refrigerator for 1 hour.
2. Place a single layer of chicken slices in both the drawers. Then, install the crisper plate in the drawer on top of the chicken slices and place another layer of chicken slices on the crisper plate. Insert the drawers into the unit.
3. Select zone 1, select Dehydrate, set the temperature to 60 C, and set the time to 7 hours.
4. Select the Match button to copy the zone 1 settings to zone 2.
5. Press the Start/Stop to begin cooking.

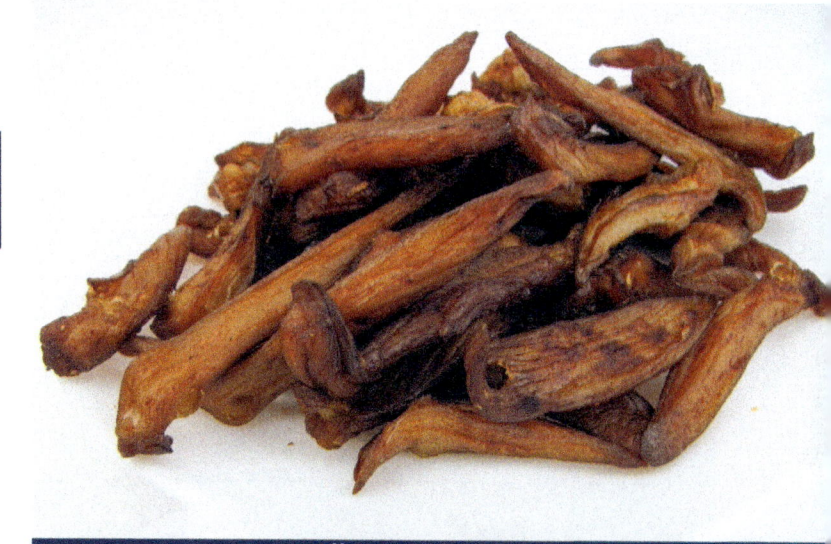

Ingredients Required:
Serving: 4

- Chicken tenders, boneless & cut into 1/4-inch slices - 700 g
- Soy sauce - 120 ml
- Ground ginger - 1/4 tsp
- Black pepper - 1/4 tsp
- Garlic powder - 1/2 tsp
- Lemon juice - 1 tsp

Per Person: Calories 229, Carbs 12.2g, Fat 6.45g, Protein 30.91g

This page is for your notes

Meat Recipes

Meatballs

Procedure of Cooking:
Cooking Period: 10 mins.

1. Add ground beef and remaining ingredients into the mixing bowl and mix until well combined.
2. Make equal shapes of balls from the meat mixture.
3. Install a crisper plate in both drawers, then place half of the meatballs in the zone 1 drawer and half in the zone 2 drawer, then insert the drawers into the unit.
4. Select zone 1, select Air Fry, set the temperature to 200 C, and set the time to 10 minutes.
5. Select the Match button to copy the zone 1 settings to zone 2.
6. Press the Start/Stop to begin cooking.
7. Serve and enjoy.

Ingredients Required:
Serving: 4

- Egg, lightly beaten - 1
- Ground beef - 500 g
- Milk - 2 tbsp
- Italian seasoning - 1 tsp
- Parsley, chopped - 2 tbsp
- Breadcrumbs - 50 g
- Parmesan cheese, grated - 10 g
- Pepper
- Salt

Per Person: Calories 372, Carbs 8.43g, Fat 20.98g, Protein 34.92g

Parmesan Pork Chops

Procedure of Cooking:
Cooking Period: 18 mins.

1. In a bowl, mix parmesan cheese, dried herbs, mustard, onion powder, garlic powder, paprika, pepper, and salt.
2. Brush the pork chops with oil and coat with the parmesan cheese mixture.
3. Install a crisper plate in both drawers, then place half of the pork chops in the zone 1 drawer and half in the zone 2 drawer, then insert the drawers into the unit.
4. Select zone 1, select Air Fry, set the temperature to 200 C, and set the time to 18 minutes.
5. Select the Match button to copy the zone 1 settings to zone 2.
6. Press the Start/Stop to begin cooking.
7. Flip the pork chops after 12 minutes.
8. Serve and enjoy.

Ingredients Required:
Serving: 4

- Pork chops, bone-in - 4
- Parmesan cheese, grated - 50 g
- Dried herbs - 1/2 tsp
- Ground mustard - 1 tsp
- Onion powder - 1 tsp
- Garlic powder - 2 tsp
- Smoked paprika - 1 tsp
- Pepper - 1/2 tsp
- Salt - 1 tsp
- Olive oil - 2 tbsp

Per Person: Calories 431, Carbs 2.3g, Fat 26.2g, Protein 41.9g

Quick Pork Chop Bites

Procedure of Cooking:
Cooking Period: 6 mins.

1. In a mixing bowl, toss pork chop pieces with the remaining ingredients until well coated.
2. Install a crisper plate in both drawers, then add half of the pork chop pieces in the zone 1 drawer and half in the zone 2 drawer, then insert the drawers into the unit.
3. Select zone 1, select Air Fry, set the temperature to 200 C, and set the time to 6 minutes.
4. Select the Match button to copy the zone 1 settings to zone 2.
5. Press the Start/Stop to begin cooking.
6. Serve and enjoy.

Ingredients Required:
Serving: 4

- Pork chops cut into ½-inch pieces - 4
- Dried thyme - 1 tsp
- Paprika - ¼ tsp
- Garlic powder - ¼ tsp
- Onion powder - ½ tsp
- Olive oil - 1 tbsp
- Pepper
- Salt

Per Person: Calories 365, Carbs 1.58g, Fat 20.79g, Protein 40.53g

Quick Beef Skewers

Procedure of Cooking:
Cooking Period: 8 mins.

1. Add meat pieces and remaining ingredients into the mixing bowl and mix well. Cover and place in refrigerator for overnight.
2. Thread marinated steak pieces onto the skewers.
3. Install a crisper plate in both drawers, then place half skewers in the zone 1 drawer and half in the zone 2 drawer, and then insert the drawers into the unit.
4. Select zone 1, select Air Fry, set the temperature to 200 C, and set the time to 8 minutes.
5. Select the Match button to copy the zone 1 settings to zone 2.
6. Press the Start/Stop to begin cooking.
7. Turn skewers halfway through.
8. Serve and enjoy.

Ingredients Required:
Serving: 4

- Sirloin steak cut into 1-inch chunks - 680 g
- Cumin - 1/2 tsp
- Sweet pepper, cut into pieces - 1
- Garlic cloves, minced - 3
- Olive oil - 60 ml
- Chili powder - 1/2 tsp
- Lemon juice - 1 tbsp
- Onion, cut into pieces - 1
- Pepper
- Salt

Per Person: Calories 467, Carbs 6g, Fat 32.63g, Protein 36.16g

Steak Bites with Veggies

Procedure of Cooking:
Cooking Period: 20 mins.

1. In a mixing bowl, mix steak strips with melted butter, garlic, onion, sweet pepper, mushrooms, pepper, and salt.
2. Install a crisper plate in both drawers, then place half of the steak mixture in the zone 1 drawer and half in the zone 2 drawer, then insert the drawers into the unit.
3. Select zone 1, select Air Fry, set the temperature to 200 C, and set the time to 20 minutes.
4. Select the Match button to copy the zone 1 settings to zone 2.
5. Press the Start/Stop to begin cooking.
6. Stir the steak-veggie mixture halfway through.
7. Serve and enjoy.

Ingredients Required:
Serving: 4

- Egg, lightly beaten - 1
- Ribeye steak, cut into strips - 450 g
- Garlic cloves, minced - 2
- Butter, melted - 2 tbsp
- Onion, sliced - 1/2
- Sweet pepper, chopped - 1
- Mushrooms, quartered - 220 g
- Pepper
- Salt

Per Person: Calories 665, Carbs 156.7g, Fat 7.52g, Protein 20.78g

Tasty Steak Strips

Procedure of Cooking:
Cooking Period: 10 mins.

1. In a bowl, mix steak strips with remaining ingredients until well coated.
2. Install a crisper plate in both drawers, then add half of the steak strips in the zone 1 drawer and half in the zone 2 drawer, then insert the drawers into the unit.
3. Select zone 1, select Air Fry, set the temperature to 200 C, and set the time to 10 minutes.
4. Select the Match button to copy the zone 1 settings to zone 2.
5. Press the Start/Stop to begin cooking.
6. Stir the meat mixture halfway through.
7. Serve and enjoy.

Ingredients Required:
Serving: 4

- Sirloin steak strips - 450 g
- Onion powder - 1 tsp
- Garlic powder - 1 tsp
- Brown sugar - 2 tbsp
- Olive oil - 1 tbsp
- Pepper
- Salt

Per Person: Calories 253, Carbs 2.17g, Fat 16.49g, Protein 23.88g

Juicy Pork Chops

Procedure of Cooking:
Cooking Period: 10 mins.

1. In a small bowl, mix the olive oil, paprika, garlic powder, onion powder, dried herbs, pepper, and salt.
2. Brush pork chops with the oil spice mixture.
3. Install a crisper plate in both drawers, then place half of the pork chops in the zone 1 drawer and half in the zone 2 drawer, then insert the drawers into the unit.
4. Select zone 1, select Air Fry, set the temperature to 190 C, and set the time to 10 minutes.
5. Select the Match button to copy the zone 1 settings to zone 2.
6. Press the Start/Stop to begin cooking.
7. Flip the pork chops halfway through.
8. Serve and enjoy.

Ingredients Required:
Serving: 4

- Pork chops, boneless - 4
- Dried herbs - 1 tsp
- Onion powder - 1 tsp
- Garlic powder - 1 tsp
- Paprika - 1 tsp
- Olive oil - 2 tbsp
- Pepper
- Salt

Per Person: Calories 400, Carbs 2.3g, Fat 24.4g, Protein 40.9g

Juicy Pork Meatballs

Procedure of Cooking:
Cooking Period: 15 mins.

1. In a mixing bowl, mix ground pork, onion, garlic powder, smoked paprika, mustard powder, pepper, and salt until well combined.
2. Make equal shapes of balls from the meat mixture.
3. Install a crisper plate in both drawers, then place half of the meatballs in the zone 1 drawer and half in the zone 2 drawer, then insert the drawers into the unit.
4. Select zone 1, select Air Fry, set the temperature to 190 C, and set the time to 15 minutes.
5. Select the Match button to copy the zone 1 settings to zone 2.
6. Press the Start/Stop to begin cooking.
7. Turn the meatballs halfway through.
8. Serve and enjoy.

Ingredients Required:
Serving: 4

- Ground pork - 450 g
- Mustard powder - ½ tsp
- Smoked paprika - 1 tsp
- Garlic powder - 1 tsp
- Onion, chopped - ½
- Pepper
- Salt

Per Person: Calories 317, Carbs 3.26g, Fat 20.17g, Protein 29g

Simple Lamb Skewers

Procedure of Cooking:
Cooking Period: 10 mins.

1. Add the meat pieces and remaining ingredients into the bowl and mix until well combined. Cover and set aside for 15 minutes.
2. Thread the marinated meat pieces onto the skewers.
3. Install a crisper plate in both drawers, then place half of the skewers in the zone 1 drawer and half in the zone 2 drawer, and then insert the drawers into the unit.
4. Select zone 1, select Air Fry, set the temperature to 180 C, and set the time to 10 minutes.
5. Select the Match button to copy the zone 1 settings to zone 2.
6. Press the Start/Stop to begin cooking.
7. Turn the skewers halfway through.
8. Serve and enjoy.

Ingredients Required:
Serving: 4

- Lamb shoulder chops, cut into 1-inch pieces - 450 g
- Fennel seed, crushed - 1 tsp
- Ground cumin - 1 tbsp
- Red chili flakes, crushed - 1 tbsp
- Dry sherry - 2 tsp
- Olive oil - 1 tbsp
- Granulated garlic - 2 tsp
- Kosher salt - 1 tsp

Per Person: Calories 233, Carbs 2.97g, Fat 14.36g, Protein 24.06g

Pork Chops with Sprouts

Procedure of Cooking:
Cooking Period: 10 mins.

1. Add pork chops and Brussels sprouts into the mixing bowl.
2. In a small bowl, mix oil, maple syrup, Dijon mustard, pepper, and salt. Pour over the pork chop sprout mixture and mix well.
3. Install a crisper plate in both drawers, then add half of the pork chop sprout mixture in the zone 1 drawer and half in the zone 2 drawer, then insert the drawers into the unit.
4. Select zone 1, select Air Fry, set the temperature to 200 C, and set the time to 10 minutes.
5. Select the Match button to copy the zone 1 settings to zone 2.
6. Press the Start/Stop to begin cooking.
7. Serve and enjoy.

Ingredients Required:
Serving: 4

- Pork chops - 4
- Brussels sprouts, quartered - 350 g
- Maple syrup - 1 tsp
- Olive oil - 1 tsp
- Dijon mustard - 1 tsp
- Pepper
- Salt

Per Person: Calories 384, Carbs 9.86g, Fat 18.81g, Protein 43.35g

Steak with Vegetables

Procedure of Cooking:
Cooking Period: 8 mins.

1. In a bowl, toss steak cubes with mushrooms, butter, broccoli, soy sauce, garlic, pepper, and salt.
2. Install a crisper plate in both drawers, then add half of the steak-vegetable mixture in the zone 1 drawer and half in the zone 2 drawer, then insert the drawers into the unit.
3. Select zone 1, select Air Fry, set the temperature to 200 C, and set the time to 8 minutes.
4. Select the Match button to copy the zone 1 settings to zone 2.
5. Press the Start/Stop to begin cooking.
6. Stir the steak-vegetable mixture halfway through.
7. Serve and enjoy.

Ingredients Required:
Serving: 4

- Ribeye steak, cut into cubes - 450 g
- Broccoli florets - 350 g
- Butter, melted - 2 tbsp
- Mushrooms, sliced - 230 g
- Garlic cloves, minced - 4
- Soy sauce, low-sodium - 1 tsp
- Pepper
- Salt

Per Person: Calories 417, Carbs 45.7g, Fat 15.98g, Protein 30.95g

Marinated Flank Steak

Procedure of Cooking:
Cooking Period: 10 mins.

1. Add flank steak and remaining ingredients into the large mixing bowl and mix well. Cover and set aside for 50 minutes.
2. Install a crisper plate in both drawers, then place half of the steaks in the zone 1 drawer and half in the zone 2 drawer, then insert the drawers into the unit.
3. Select zone 1, select Air Fry, set the temperature to 180 C, and set the time to 10 minutes.
4. Select the Match button to copy the zone 1 settings to zone 2.
5. Press the Start/Stop to begin cooking.
6. Flip the steaks halfway through.
7. Serve and enjoy.

Ingredients Required:
Serving: 4

- Flank steak - 4
- Garlic, minced - 1 tsp
- Red wine vinegar - 60 ml
- Olive oil - 60 ml
- Dijon mustard - 1 tbsp
- Worcestershire sauce - 1 tbsp
- Soy sauce, low-sodium - 1 tbsp
- Pepper
- Salt

Per Person: Calories 315, Carbs 3.4g, Fat 15.6g, Protein 37.2g

Pork Belly Bites with Mushrooms

Procedure of Cooking:
Cooking Period: 15 mins.

1. In a mixing bowl, toss pork belly cubes with the remaining ingredients until well coated.
2. Install a crisper plate in both drawers, then add half meat mixture in the zone 1 drawer and half in the zone 2 drawer, and then insert the drawers into the unit.
3. Select zone 1, select Air Fry, set the temperature to 200 C, and set the time to 15 minutes.
4. Select the Match button to copy the zone 1 settings to zone 2.
5. Press the Start/Stop to begin cooking.
6. Stir the meat mixture halfway through.
7. Serve and enjoy.

Ingredients Required:
Serving: 4

- Pork belly, cut into 3/4-inch cubes - 450 g
- Garlic powder - 1/2 tsp
- Mushrooms, cleaned and halved - 230 g
- Soy sauce, low-sodium - 1 tsp
- Olive oil - 2 tbsp
- Pepper
- Salt

Per Person: Calories 540, Carbs 44.42g, Fat 27.61g, Protein 34.21g

Lemon Herb Lamb Chops

Procedure of Cooking:
Cooking Period: 6 mins.

1. Add lamb chops and remaining ingredients into the large mixing bowl and mix well. Cover and place in refrigerator for 30 minutes.
2. Install a crisper plate in both drawers, then place half of the lamb chops in the zone 1 drawer and half in the zone 2 drawer, then insert the drawers into the unit.
3. Select zone 1, select Air Fry, set the temperature to 200 C, and set the time to 6 minutes.
4. Select the Match button to copy the zone 1 settings to zone 2.
5. Press the Start/Stop to begin cooking.
6. Serve and enjoy.

Ingredients Required:
Serving: 8

- Lamb chops - 8
- Olive oil - 60 ml
- Thyme, chopped - 1 tbsp
- Garlic cloves, minced - 3
- Lemon zest, grated - 1
- Rosemary, chopped - 1 tbsp
- Dried oregano - 1/2 tsp
- Lemon juice - 2 tbsp
- Pepper
- Salt

Per Person: Calories 244, Carbs 1.74g, Fat 15.41g, Protein 25.22g

Baked Beef Meatballs

Procedure of Cooking:
Cooking Period: 30 mins.

1. Add ground beef and remaining ingredients into the large bowl and mix until well combined.
2. Make equal shapes of balls from the meat mixture.
3. Install a crisper plate in both drawers, then place half meatballs in the zone 1 drawer and half in the zone 2 drawer, then insert the drawers into the unit.
4. Select zone 1, select Bake, set the temperature to 180 C, and set the time to 30 minutes.
5. Select the Match button to copy the zone 1 settings to zone 2.
6. Press the Start/Stop to begin cooking.
7. Turn the meatballs halfway through.
8. Serve and enjoy.

Ingredients Required:
Serving: 24 meatballs

- Eggs, lightly beaten - 2
- Ground beef - 450 g
- Parsley, chopped - 12 g
- Dried oregano - ½ tsp
- Garlic cloves, minced - 3
- Onion, minced - 1
- Breadcrumbs - 60 g
- Parmesan cheese, grated - 45 g
- Pepper
- Salt

Per Person: Calories 71, Carbs 2.08g, Fat 4.09g, Protein 6.25g

Steak with Potatoes

Procedure of Cooking:
Cooking Period: 20 mins.

1. Add the potatoes to the boiling water and cook for 5 minutes. Drain well.
2. Add the steak cubes, potatoes, and remaining ingredients into the mixing bowl and toss well.
3. Install a crisper plate in both drawers, then add half steak potato mixture in the zone 1 drawer and half in the zone 2 drawer, then insert the drawers into the unit.
4. Select zone 1, select Air Fry, set the temperature to 200 C, and set the time to 15 minutes.
5. Select the Match button to copy the zone 1 settings to zone 2.
6. Press the Start/Stop to begin cooking.
7. Stir the steak-potato mixture halfway through.
8. Serve and enjoy.

Ingredients Required:
Serving: 4

- Steaks, cut into 1/2-inch cubes - 450 g
- Potatoes, cut into 1/2-inch cubes - 230 g
- Butter, melted - 2 tbsp
- Garlic powder - 1/2 tsp
- Soy sauce, low-sodium - 1 tsp
- Pepper
- Salt

Per Person: Calories 260, Carbs 39.09g, Fat 9.95g, Protein 4.31g

Quick Steak Bites

Procedure of Cooking:
Cooking Period: 10 mins.

1. Add steak pieces and remaining ingredients into the mixing bowl and mix well. Cover and let it marinate for 30 minutes.
2. Remove steak pieces from the marinade.
3. Install a crisper plate in both drawers, then place half of the steak pieces in the zone 1 drawer and half in the zone 2 drawer, then insert the drawers into the unit.
4. Select zone 1, select Air Fry, set the temperature to 200 C, and set the time to 10 minutes.
5. Select the Match button to copy the zone 1 settings to zone 2.
6. Press the Start/Stop to begin cooking.
7. Turn the steak pieces halfway through.
8. Serve and enjoy.

Ingredients Required:
Serving: 6

- Ribeye steak, cut into pieces - 450 g
- Red pepper flakes, crushed - 1/4 tsp
- Garlic powder - 1/2 tsp
- Lemon juice - 1 tbsp
- Lemon zest - 1 tbsp
- Parsley, chopped - 1 tbsp
- Soy sauce, low-sodium - 1/2 tsp
- Dijon mustard - 1/2 tbsp
- Butter, melted - 120 g
- Pepper
- Salt

Per Person: Calories 129, Carbs 1.66g, Fat 6.35g, Protein 16.56g

Sausage with Vegetables

Procedure of Cooking:
Cooking Period: 10 mins.

1. Add sausage slices and remaining ingredients into the mixing bowl and mix everything well.
2. Install a crisper plate in both drawers, then add half of the sausage-vegetable mixture in the zone 1 drawer and half in the zone 2 drawer, then insert the drawers into the unit.
3. Select zone 1, select Air Fry, set the temperature to 190 C, and set the time to 10 minutes.
4. Select the Match button to copy the zone 1 settings to zone 2.
5. Press the Start/Stop to begin cooking.
6. Stir the sausage-vegetable mixture halfway through.
7. Serve and enjoy.

Ingredients Required:
Serving: 4

- Smoked sausage, sliced - 450 g
- Cajun seasoning - 1 tbsp
- Olive oil - 1 tbsp
- Mushrooms, quartered - 100 g
- Onion, quartered - 1 medium
- Courgetti, quartered - 150 g
- Squash, quartered - 125 g
- Pepper
- Salt

Per Person: Calories 429, Carbs 37.05g, Fat 24.34g, Protein 24.3g

Pork Jerky

Procedure of Cooking:
Cooking Period: 5 hours

1. Add meat slices and remaining ingredients into the zip-lock bag, seal the bag, and place in the refrigerator overnight.
2. Place a single layer of pork slices in both the drawers. Then, install the crisper plate in the drawer on top of the pork slices and place another layer of pork slices on the crisper plate. Insert the drawers into the unit.
3. Select zone 1, select Dehydrate, set the temperature to 70 C, and set the time to 5 hours.
4. Select the Match button to copy the zone 1 settings to zone 2.
5. Press the Start/Stop to begin cooking.

Ingredients Required:
Serving: 4

- Pork lean meat, sliced thinly - 450 g
- Chili powder - 1 tsp
- Paprika - 1 tsp
- Garlic powder - 1/2 tsp
- Pepper - 1/4 tsp
- Oregano - 1/2 tsp
- Salt - 1 tsp

Per Person: Calories 149, Carbs 2.51g, Fat 4.47g, Protein 25.86g

Beef Jerky

Procedure of Cooking:
Cooking Period: 8 hours

1. Add steak slices and remaining ingredients into the mixing bowl and mix well, cover, and place in the refrigerator overnight.
2. Place a single layer of steak slices in both the drawers. Then, install the crisper plate in the drawer on top of the steak slices and place another layer of steak slices on the crisper plate. Insert the drawers into the unit.
3. Select zone 1, select Dehydrate, set the temperature to 60 C, and set the time to 8 hours.
4. Select the Match button to copy the zone 1 settings to zone 2.
5. Press the Start/Stop to begin cooking.

Ingredients Required:
Serving: 6

- Flank steak, cut into thin slices - 900 g
- Soy sauce - 180 ml
- Cayenne - 1/4 tsp
- Liquid smoke - 1 tsp
- Red pepper flakes - 1 1/2 tbsp
- Ranch seasoning - 3 tbsp
- Worcestershire sauce - 177 ml

Per Person: Calories 605, Carbs 18.21g, Fat 44.23g, Protein 33.34g

This page is for your notes

Sausages — upper Crisper Plate 200c 8-11m

Vegetable Recipes

Healthy Root Vegetable

Procedure of Cooking:
Cooking Period: 35 mins.

1. In a mixing bowl, toss root vegetables with olive oil, pepper, and salt until well coated.
2. Install a crisper plate in both drawers, then add half of the root vegetables in the zone 1 drawer and the remaining half in the zone 2 drawer, then insert the drawers into the unit.
3. Select zone 1, select Air Fry, set the temperature to 170 C, and set the time to 25 minutes.
4. Select the Match button to copy the zone 1 settings to zone 2.
5. Press the Start/Stop to begin cooking.
6. Transfer the root vegetables to a large mixing bowl. Add rosemary, garlic, and red wine vinegar to the vegetables and toss well.
7. Return the vegetables to the air fryer drawers and cook for 10 minutes more at 190 C.
8. Serve and enjoy.

Ingredients Required:
Serving: 4

- Root vegetables cut into 2-inch chunks - 650 g
- Rosemary sprigs, chopped - 2
- Garlic cloves, peeled & sliced - 4
- Olive oil - 1 tbsp
- Red wine vinegar - 1 tbsp
- Pepper
- Salt

Per Person: Calories 107, Carbs 19.45g, Fat 3.46g, Protein 0.44g

Garlic Lime Courgette

Procedure of Cooking:
Cooking Period: 15 mins.

1. In a mixing bowl, mix together courgette slices, garlic granules, olive oil, onion, pepper, and salt.
2. Install a crisper plate in both drawers, then add half the vegetable mixture in the zone 1 drawer and half in the zone 2 drawer, then insert the drawers into the unit.
3. Select zone 1, select Air Fry, set the temperature to 200 C, and set the time to 15 minutes.
4. Select the Match button to copy the zone 1 settings to zone 2.
5. Press the Start/Stop to begin cooking.
6. Stir the vegetables halfway through.
7. Transfer the roasted vegetables into a bowl and stir in lime juice.
8. Serve and enjoy.

Ingredients Required:
Serving: 4

- Courgette, cut into ½-inch thick slices - 500 g
- Lime juice - 2 tbsp
- Garlic granules - 1 tsp
- Olive oil - 1 tsp
- Onion, sliced - 1
- Pepper - ¼ tsp
- Salt - ½ tsp

Per Person: Calories 36, Carbs 5.23g, Fat 1.54g, Protein 1.67g

Roasted Mixed Vegetables

Procedure of Cooking:
Cooking Period: 20 mins.

1. In a large bowl, toss all vegetables with garlic granules, thyme, rosemary, olive oil, pepper, and salt until well coated.
2. Install a crisper plate in both drawers, then add half of the vegetable mixture in the zone 1 drawer and half in the zone 2 drawer, then insert the drawers into the unit.
3. Select zone 1, select Air Fry, set the temperature to 200 C, and set the time to 20 minutes.
4. Select the Match button to copy the zone 1 settings to zone 2.
5. Press the Start/Stop to begin cooking.
6. Stir the vegetables halfway through.
7. Serve and enjoy.

Ingredients Required:
Serving: 4

- Red sweet pepper, cut into 1-inch pieces - 1
- Courgetti, cut into 1-inch pieces - 1
- Carrot, peeled & cut into 1-inch pieces - 1
- Onion, cut into 1-inch pieces - 1
- Garlic granules - ½ tsp
- Dried thyme - ½ tsp
- Dried rosemary - ½ tsp
- Olive oil - 1 tbsp
- Pepper - ¼ tsp
- Sea salt - ½ tsp

Per Person: Calories 54, Carbs 5.61g, Fat 3.51g, Protein 0.83g

Roasted Brussels Sprouts

Procedure of Cooking:
Cooking Period: 20 mins.

1. Add steak slices and remaining ingredients into the In a mixing bowl, toss the Brussels sprouts with pancetta, oil, chestnuts, pepper, and salt until well coated.
2. Install a crisper plate in both drawers, then add half of the Brussels sprout mixture in the zone 1 drawer and half in the zone 2 drawer, then insert the drawers into the unit.
3. Select zone 1, select Air Fry, set the temperature to 180 C, and set the time to 20 minutes.
4. Select the Match button to copy the zone 1 settings to zone 2.
5. Press the Start/Stop to begin cooking.
6. Stir the Brussels sprout mixture halfway through.
7. Serve and enjoy.

Ingredients Required:
Serving: 4

- Brussels sprouts, trimmed & halved - 500 g
- Pancetta, chopped - 100 g
- Olive oil - 1 tbsp
- Chestnuts, halved - 180 g
- Pepper
- Salt

Per Person: Calories 236, Carbs 32.74g, Fat 7.55g, Protein 11.94g

Crispy Broccoli Bites

Procedure of Cooking:
Cooking Period: 20 mins.

1. Add broccoli florets and remaining ingredients into the mixing bowl and toss well.
2. Install a crisper plate in both drawers, then add half of the broccoli florets in the zone 1 drawer and half in the zone 2 drawer, then insert the drawers into the unit.
3. Select zone 1, select Bake, set the temperature to 200 C, and set the time to 20 minutes.
4. Select the Match button to copy the zone 1 settings to zone 2.
5. Press the Start/Stop to begin cooking.
6. Stir the broccoli halfway through.
7. Serve and enjoy.

Ingredients Required:
Serving: 4

- Broccoli florets - 525 g
- Garlic powder - ¼ tsp
- Nutritional yeast - 15 g
- Olive oil - 2 tbsp
- Cayenne pepper - ¼ tsp
- Almond flour - 25 g
- Salt - ¼ tsp

Per Person: Calories 101, Carbs 4.76g, Fat 7.12g, Protein 5.31g

Roasted Cauliflower

Procedure of Cooking:
Cooking Period: 20 mins.

1. In a mixing bowl, toss cauliflower florets, tomatoes, oil, pepper, and salt.
2. Install a crisper plate in both drawers, then place half of the cauliflower-tomato mixture in the zone 1 drawer and half in the zone 2 drawer, and insert the drawers into the unit.
3. Select zone 1, select Roast, set the temperature to 200 C, and set the time to 20 minutes.
4. Select the Match button to copy the zone 1 settings to zone 2.
5. Press the Start/Stop to begin cooking.
6. Stir the cauliflower-tomato mixture halfway through.
7. Serve and enjoy.

Ingredients Required:
Serving: 4

- Cauliflower florets - 1300 g
- Cherry tomatoes, halved - 114 g
- Olive oil - 3 tbsp
- Pepper
- Salt

Per Person: Calories 121, Carbs 6.55g, Fat 10.45g, Protein 2.29g

Sweet Potato Courgette Patties

Procedure of Cooking:
Cooking Period: 10 mins.

1. In a mixing bowl, add the shredded courgette, shredded sweet potato, and remaining ingredients and mix until well combined.
2. Make equal shapes of patties from the mixture.
3. Install a crisper plate in both drawers, then place half of the patties in the zone 1 drawer and half in the zone 2 drawer, then insert the drawers into the unit.
4. Select zone 1, select Air Fry, set the temperature to 190 C, and set the time to 10 minutes.
5. Select the Match button to copy the zone 1 settings to zone 2.
6. Press the Start/Stop to begin cooking.
7. Serve and enjoy.

Ingredients Required:
Serving: 6

- Egg, lightly beaten - 1
- Sweet potato, peeled & shredded - 1
- Courgette, shredded & excess liquid squeezed out - 2
- Baking powder - ½ tsp
- Garlic powder - ½ tsp
- Italian seasoning - 1 tsp
- Flour - 30 g
- Kosher salt - 1 tsp

Per Person: Calories 33, Carbs 2.44g, Fat 1.74g, Protein 2.09g

Aubergine Slices

Procedure of Cooking:
Cooking Period: 4 hours

1. In a bowl, toss aubergine slices with paprika and garlic powder.
2. Place a single layer of aubergine slices in both the drawers. Then, install the crisper plate in the drawer on top of the aubergine slices and place another layer of aubergine slices on the crisper plate. Insert the drawers into the unit.
3. Select zone 1, select Dehydrate, set the temperature to 60 C, and set the time to 4 hours.
4. Select the Match button to copy the zone 1 settings to zone 2.
5. Press the Start/Stop to begin cooking.

Ingredients Required:
Serving: 4

- Medium aubergine, cut into ¼-inch thick slices - 2
- Paprika - 1 tsp
- Garlic powder - ¼ tsp

Per Person: Calories 71, Carbs 16.57g, Fat 0.57g, Protein 2.8g

Green Bean Chips

Procedure of Cooking:
Cooking Period: 8 hours

1. In a mixing bowl, toss green beans with onion powder, olive oil, garlic powder, and salt.
2. Place a single layer of green beans in both the drawers. Then, install the crisper plate in the drawer on top of the green beans and place another layer of green beans on the crisper plate. Insert the drawers into the unit.
3. Select zone 1, select Dehydrate, set the temperature to 60 C, and set the time to 8 hours.
4. Select the Match button to copy the zone 1 settings to zone 2.
5. Press the Start/Stop to begin cooking.

Ingredients Required:
Serving: 4

- Green beans, frozen & thawed - 900 g
- Onion powder - ½ tsp
- Olive oil - 2 tbsp
- Garlic powder - ½ tsp
- Salt - 2 tsp

Per Person: Calories 146, Carbs 17.1g, Fat 7.21g, Protein 3.27g

Beet Slices

Procedure of Cooking:
Cooking Period: 8 hours

1. Season beet slices with salt.
2. Place a single layer of beet slices in both the drawers. Then, install the crisper plate in the drawer on top of the beet slices and place another layer of beet slices on the crisper plate. Insert the drawers into the unit.
3. Select zone 1, select Dehydrate, set the temperature to 60 C, and set the time to 8 hours.
4. Select the Match button to copy the zone 1 settings to zone 2.
5. Press the Start/Stop to begin cooking.

Ingredients Required:
Serving: 4

- Medium beets, peeled and sliced - 4
- Salt - 1 tbsp

Per Person: Calories 35, Carbs 7.84g, Fat 0.14g, Protein 1.32g

Desserts

Cranberry Muffins

Procedure of Cooking:
Cooking Period: 20 mins.

1. In a mixing bowl, mix almond flour, cinnamon, baking powder, and coconut flour.
2. In a separate bowl, whisk eggs with butter, sweetener, heavy cream, vanilla, and orange zest until frothy.
3. Pour the egg mixture into the almond flour mixture and mix until just combined. Add cranberries and fold well.
4. Spoon batter into the silicone muffin molds.
5. Install a crisper plate in both drawers, then place half of the muffin molds in the zone 1 drawer and half in the zone 2 drawer, then insert the drawers into the unit.
6. Select zone 1, select Bake, set the temperature to 180 C, and set the time to 20 minutes.
7. Select the Match button to copy the zone 1 settings to zone 2.
8. Press the Start/Stop to begin cooking.
9. Serve and enjoy.

Ingredients Required:
Serving: 12

- Eggs - 5
- Coconut flour - 2 tbsp
- Almond flour - 192 g
- Orange zest - 1 tbsp
- Cranberries, chopped - 90 g
- Cinnamon - 1/2 tsp
- Butter, melted - 3 tbsp
- Erythritol - 170 g
- Baking powder - 1 1/2 tsp
- Vanilla - 1 tsp
- Heavy cream - 3 tbsp

Per Person: Calories 105, Carbs 3.38g, Fat 8.41g, Protein 3.92g

Healthy Brownie Bites

Procedure of Cooking:
Cooking Period: 30 mins.

1. In a medium bowl, mix coconut flour, cocoa powder, baking soda, and sea salt.
2. In a mixing bowl, whisk together eggs, water, melted oil, and honey.
3. Slowly add the coconut flour mixture to the egg mixture and mix until well combined.
4. Spoon batter into the silicone muffin molds.
5. Install a crisper plate in both drawers, then place half of the muffin molds in the zone 1 drawer and half in the zone 2 drawer, then insert the drawers into the unit.
6. Select zone 1, select Bake, set the temperature to 180 C, and set the time to 30 minutes.
7. Select the Match button to copy the zone 1 settings to zone 2.
8. Press the Start/Stop to begin cooking.
9. Serve and enjoy.

Ingredients Required:
Serving: 9

- Eggs - 5
- Coconut flour - 60 g
- Honey - 120 ml
- Unsweetened cocoa powder - 50 g
- Baking soda - 1/2 tsp
- Water - 2 tbsp
- Coconut oil, melted - 80 ml
- Sea salt - 1/8 tsp

Per Person: Calories 211, Carbs 19.36g, Fat 14g, Protein 6g

Chocolate Muffins

Procedure of Cooking:
Cooking Period: 15 mins.

1. In a bowl, whisk egg, oil, vinegar, brown sugar, vanilla, and milk.
2. Add flour, espresso powder, baking soda, cocoa powder, baking powder, and salt and stir until well combined.
3. Pour batter into the silicone muffin molds.
4. Install a crisper plate in both drawers, then place half of the muffin molds in the zone 1 drawer and half in the zone 2 drawer, then insert the drawers into the unit.
5. Select zone 1, select Air Fry, set the temperature to 180 C, and set the time to 15 minutes.
6. Select the Match button to copy the zone 1 settings to zone 2.
7. Press the Start/Stop to begin cooking.
8. Serve and enjoy.

Ingredients Required:
Serving: 8

- Egg - 1
- All-purpose flour - 120 g
- Espresso powder - 1/2 tsp
- Baking powder - 1/2 tsp
- Cocoa powder - 50 g
- Brown sugar - 160 g
- Vegetable oil - 80 ml
- Apple cider vinegar - 1 tsp
- Vanilla - 1 tsp
- Milk - 180 ml
- Baking soda - 1/2 tsp
- Salt - 1/2 tsp

Per Person: Calories 257, Carbs 36.8g, Fat 11.8g, Protein 4.45g

Roasted Oranges

Procedure of Cooking:
Cooking Period: 5 mins.

1. In a small bowl, mix cinnamon and brown sugar and sprinkle on the cut side of the oranges.
2. Install a crisper plate in both drawers, then place half of the oranges in the zone 1 drawer and half in the zone 2 drawer, then insert the drawers into the unit.
3. Select zone 1, select Air Fry, set the temperature to 200 C, and set the time to 5 minutes.
4. Select the Match button to copy the zone 1 settings to zone 2.
5. Press the Start/Stop to begin cooking.
6. Serve and enjoy.

Ingredients Required:
Serving: 6

- Oranges, cut in half - 6
- Cinnamon - ¾ tsp
- Brown sugar - 3 tsp

Per Person: Calories 78, Carbs 18.68g, Fat 0.17g, Protein 0.97g

Brazilan Pineapple Chunks

Procedure of Cooking:
Cooking Period: 10 mins.

1. In a bowl, mix pineapple, honey, lime juice, and brown sugar. Cover and place in the refrigerator for 1 hour.
2. Install a crisper plate in both drawers, then add half of the pineapple chunks in the zone 1 drawer and half in the zone 2 drawer, then insert the drawers into the unit.
3. Select zone 1, select Air Fry, set the temperature to 200 C, and set the time to 10 minutes.
4. Select the Match button to copy the zone 1 settings to zone 2.
5. Press the Start/Stop to begin cooking.
6. Stir the pineapple chunks halfway through.
7. Serve and enjoy.

Ingredients Required:
Serving: 4

- Pineapple chunks - 560 g
- Honey - 3 tbsp
- Lime juice - 2 tbsp
- Brown sugar - 50 g

Per Person: Calories 224, Carbs 58.57g, Fat 0.15g, Protein 0.66g

Cinnamon Figs

Procedure of Cooking:
Cooking Period: 10 mins.

1. In a small bowl, mix sugar and cinnamon.
2. Dip each fig cut side in the sugar mixture.
3. Install a crisper plate in both drawers, then place half of the figs in the zone 1 drawer and half in the zone 2 drawer, then insert the drawers into the unit.
4. Select zone 1, select Air Fry, set the temperature to 200 C, and set the time to 10 minutes.
5. Select the Match button to copy the zone 1 settings to zone 2.
6. Press the Start/Stop to begin cooking.
7. Serve and enjoy.

Ingredients Required:
Serving: 4

- Fresh figs, cut in half lengthwise - 300 g
- Sugar - 4 tbsp
- Cinnamon - 1 tsp

Per Person: Calories 218, Carbs 56.09g, Fat 0.7g, Protein 2.48g

Lemon Muffins

Procedure of Cooking:
Cooking Period: 25 mins.

1. In a mixing bowl, whisk eggs with canola oil, lemon zest, and vanilla.
2. Add almond flour, baking powder, lemon juice, and sweetener and mix until just combined.
3. Add poppy seeds and fold well.
4. Spoon batter into the silicone muffin molds.
5. Install a crisper plate in both drawers, then place half of the muffin molds in the zone 1 drawer and half in the zone 2 drawer, then insert the drawers into the unit.
6. Select zone 1, select Bake, set the temperature to 180 C, and set the time to 25 minutes.
7. Select the Match button to copy the zone 1 settings to zone 2.
8. Press the Start/Stop to begin cooking.
9. Serve and enjoy.

Ingredients Required:
Serving: 9

- Eggs - 3
- Almond flour - 260 g
- Lemon zest - 1 tsp
- Canola oil - 120 ml
- Baking powder - 2 tsp
- Swerve - 100 g
- Lemon juice - 60 ml
- Poppy seeds - 1 tbsp
- Vanilla - 1 tsp

Per Person: Calories 162, Carbs 1.78g, Fat 15.94g, Protein 3.27g

Green Apple Slices

Procedure of Cooking:
Cooking Period: 8 hours

1. Add apple slices and lime juice to a bowl, toss well, and set aside for 5 minutes.
2. Place a single layer of apple slices in both the drawers. Then, install the crisper plate in the drawer on top of the apple slices and place another layer of apple slices on the crisper plate. Insert the drawers into the unit.
3. Select zone 1, select Dehydrate, set the temperature to 60 C, and set the time to 8 hours.
4. Select the Match button to copy the zone 1 settings to zone 2.
5. Press the Start/Stop to begin cooking.

Ingredients Required:
Serving: 4

- Green apples, cored & cut into 8-inch-thick slices - 4
- Fresh lime juice - 1/2

Per Person: Calories 138, Carbs 34.82g, Fat 0.88g, Protein 0.39g

Peach Slices

Procedure of Cooking:
Cooking Period: 8 hours

1. Add lemon juice and peach slices into the bowl and toss well.
2. Place a single layer of peach slices in both the drawers. Then, install the crisper plate in the drawer on top of the peach slices and place another layer of peach slices on the crisper plate. Insert the drawers into the unit.
3. Select zone 1, select Dehydrate, set the temperature to 60 C, and set the time to 8 hours.
4. Select the Match button to copy the zone 1 settings to zone 2.
5. Press the Start/Stop to begin cooking.

Ingredients Required:
Serving: 6

- Peaches, cut and remove pits, and sliced - 6
- Fresh lemon juice - 120 ml

Per Person: Calories 115, Carbs 31.31g, Fat 0.2g, Protein 0.75g

Healthy Oat Cookies

Procedure of Cooking:
Cooking Period: 15 mins.

1. In a mixing bowl, add self-raising flour and remaining ingredients and mix until well combined.
2. Make equal shapes of cookies from the mixture.
3. Install a crisper plate in both drawers, then place half of the cookies in the Zone 1 drawer and the remaining half of the cookies in the Zone 2 drawer, and then insert the drawers into the unit.
4. Select Zone 1, select Air Fry, set the temperature to 175 C, and set the time to 15 minutes.
5. Select the Match button to copy the zone 1 settings to zone 2.
6. Press the Start/Stop to begin cooking.
7. Remove cookies from the air fryer drawers and place them on a wire rack to cool completely.
8. Serve and enjoy.

Ingredients Required:
Serving: 15 cookies

- Self-raising flour - 140 g
- Sultanas - 50 g
- Baking soda - ½ tsp
- Oats - 100 g
- Ground cinnamon - 1 tsp
- Caster sugar - 100 g
- Lemon zest, grated - ½
- Golden syrup, melted - 20 g
- Butter, unsalted & melted - 85 g

Per Person: Calories 35, Carbs 7.84g, Fat 0.14g, Protein 1.32g

Conclusion

The Ninja Double Stack XL Air Fryer Cookbook is the resource you need to experience all that this amazing kitchen tool has to offer. Loaded with mouthwatering recipes, this culinary guide will help home cooks of any skill level incorporate healthier, simpler, and faster ways of cooking. Explore new flavors, enhance your health by using less oil, and cut your cooking time in half with no compromise on taste. Let this book be right by your side through your culinary journey. It is your inspiration to help you create delicious meals without much effort! Enjoy your cooking!

This page is for your notes

Carrots — lower ⅓ crispy plate 200°c 22-24 m
Cauliflower. 15-17 m
Potatoes 1 Tbsp oil lower crisp 200°c 30-35 m

This page is for your notes

Printed in Great Britain
by Amazon